What DOES the Future Hold?

Getting a Handle on the Final Events
An Overview Guide for Seventh-day Adventists

by

Kerry L. Schoonmaker

TEACH Services, Inc.
www.TEACHServices.com

Copyright © 2010 TEACH Services, Inc.
ISBN-13: 978-1-57258-596-6
Library of Congress Control Number: 2010929097

Published by
TEACH Services, Inc.
www.TEACHServices.com

"What DOES the Future Hold?" is a wonderful contribution from Kerry Schoonmaker to the community of believers, for those who love to dig deeper in the fascinating world of the Bible prophecies. He has set an example for church leaders and lay preachers, sharing his understanding of the Word of God, approaching very important issues responsibly, respecting the doctrine and the wisdom of excellent Bible Commentaries. He is an honest and sincere Christian who studies the Bible with love and dedication. Thank you Kerry, for this book, a nice example of a very spiritual ministry!
—Jose H. Cortes,
President, New Jersey Conference of Seventh-day Adventists

Kerry delights in doing Evangelism for Jesus. In his book "What DOES The Future Hold", you will become a part of his audience, experience his convictions about the approaching apocalypse, and will be better prepared to meet with your Lord.
— Leonel Pottinger
Ministerial Director, NJ Conference
Personal Ministries Director, NJ Conference

In the book, "What DOES the Future Hold", Kerry has a unique way of bringing out the close relationship which every believer in Christ should have. This relationship is the only thing we have to carry us through the days ahead. Written for Seventh-day Adventists, his thought provoking questions, along with his detailed explanations from the Bible and the Spirit of Prophecy, will cause you to deeply consider building a closer relationship with Jesus.
— Eric Garloff,
President, Sapphire Throne Media, Mt. Holly, NJ

Kerry did a wonderful job explaining the final day events leading to the second coming of Christ. This is a great book that every Seventh-Day Adventist should read.
— Roselia St. Louis,
Wesley Hills, NY

1

Kerry has been studying and preaching about the Final Events for more than two decades. Like many other students of the Bible and of the inspired word, Kerry encountered the difficulty and the confusion that surrounds this subject. Sensing the need for better understanding of this matter, Kerry felt compelled to put his findings in writing to share his insight on the subject with other people who are searching for more certainty in the understanding and sharing of the Final Events. Without claiming to have the final word on the subject or being dogmatic about it, "What DOES the Future Hold?" brings clarity to the subject of Final Events, corrects erroneous explanations and applications, and provides a proper perspective for a topic that is of such great interest among the faithful church members who desire to be ready for the Master's appearing. "What DOES the Future Holds?" is a must read and study tool for our times.

— Caesar Sprianu,
Pastor

Anyone who is a serious student and who is concerned about the future of this world can thank Kerry Schoonmaker for providing an excellent tool for clarifying The Final Events which will occur as the history of this world comes to its climax. Surveying the writings of E. G. White, Kerry brings to bear his years of study of final events and provides comments which assists the reader in appreciating the importance of developing a rational view of what is in store for the inhabitants of our world.

—Bob Comisky, pastor
Hightstown Seventh-day Adventist Church

This book is dedicated to my mother,
Betty Schoonmaker-Danko,
and in loving memory of my father,
Lee Schoonmaker.

Without their love and influence
I would not be where I am today.

CONTENTS

Chapter 1

The Close of Probation, the Seal of God & the 144,000

Introduction

W hat the Seventh-day Adventist denomination knows and under-
stands concerning the Final Events comes from two sources, the
Bible and the Spirit of Prophecy. When interpreting the Bible we have
always followed the principle of allowing the Bible to interpret itself.
As we apply this standard to every biblical subject that we study, the
Bible begins to sing to us in great harmony.

This principle must be used not only with the Bible but also with
the Spirit of Prophecy. The Spirit of Prophecy sings with understanding
when we allow it to interpret itself. Unfortunately, individuals will take
one passage from the writings of Ellen White and build a scenario from
it, rather than examining all that she received from the Lord on that
subject (out of two thousand visions) and understanding the meaning
as a whole. This practice—constructing a belief on one passage taken
out of context—leads to interpretation that is confusing, out of harmony with the rest of the Spirit of Prophecy, and full of error.

Consistent with this method of interpretation, it has been my experience, from giving seminars, that there are certain areas of the Final
Events that are somewhat misunderstood amongst Seventh-day Adventists. One of the main areas is the timing of events. For example,
many believed that we were in the time of the Shaking as far back as

the 1950s. In the 1980s friends of mine insisted we were in the time of the Shaking. In each decade since the 1950s there have been several writings from folks who believed, at that time, that we were in the time of the Shaking. However, the Spirit of Prophecy pinpoints the time of the Shaking to occur after a certain Final Event takes place that has not taken place as yet.

Another area of confusion concerning the timing of events is the timing of the Coming of Satan and his evil angels. Within one week I heard on two different Adventist television programs, from the same satellite network, two different scenarios concerning the timing of the Coming of Satan. One said it was during the Great Time of Trouble, the other before even the Little Time of Trouble. Again, the Spirit of Prophecy clearly pinpoints the timing of the beginning of this event.

As the United States went into a major economic recession in 2007-2008, many Seventh-day Adventists were running to and fro to meetings with the idea that the collapse of the U.S. economy would bring on the National Sunday Law. However, the Spirit of Prophecy clearly gives two reasons the National Sunday Law is enacted, neither of which concerns an economic collapse in the United States. In fact, the complete opposite occurs according to the Spirit of Prophecy. When the National Sunday Law is enacted in the United States, national economic ruin will follow, as we shall see.

Another area that is often misunderstood is the requirements to receive the Latter Rain. In most circles the only requirements mentioned are to pray, and be in unity, while there are many other requirements given in the Bible and Spirit of Prophecy.

These are just a few of the areas concerning the Final Events that are somewhat misunderstood!

I believe that Satan and his evil angels only need one area of error to gain a foothold and lead us down the wrong path as we approach the end of this world. Therefore, an attempt to clarify the above misunderstandings, by the grace of our Lord, Jesus Christ, as well as other issues that are misunderstood concerning the Final Events, has provided the main impetus for the writing of this book.

In this writing great care has been taken to allow the Bible and the Spirit of Prophecy to interpret themselves which will prevent errors and bring about a true understanding of the Final Events as revealed in the Bible and the Spirit of Prophecy. Of course there are no guarantees, since we continue to learn and understand more and more as we approach the end of this world. The important thing to remember is that we must allow the Bible and the Spirit of Prophecy to interpret themselves to obtain a correct understanding of the Final Events.

About This Writing

This writing is a result of more than ten years of seminars, given in many churches, on the Final Events. In each seminar, feedback was encouraged in order to bring to the forefront any additional insights given to individuals by the Holy Spirit. Those insights were prayerfully and carefully considered along with years of personal study and prayer to bring about the writing that follows. I pray, by God's grace, that this writing will be a special blessing to you and help you to be more prepared for the Final Events as we approach the end of this world.

The Texts Used

While there are many texts that describe each of the Final Events, in this book texts that best portray the events and provide the most information were selected. There are many other passages throughout the Bible and Spirit of Prophecy writings that further support these texts, and I encourage you to explore them.

With the Bible and Spirit of Prophecy texts used as the basis for this study, the chart on page 5 will give you a full picture of the Final Events. This chart will make it easier to visualize and understand these Final Events as we approach the end of this world. The events in this chart begin at the first vertical line on the left, the Judgment of the Living.

The Judgment of the Living and the Sealing

As we consider the Judgment of the Living, the first question we must ask ourselves concerning this final event is, will we know when the Judgment of the Living has begun? The answer to this question is an emphatic no! There is a particular time in history though, when the Judgment of the Dead, which started in 1844 according to biblical prophecy, will pass to the Judgment of the Living. In *The Faith I Live By*, p. 211, is the following statement: *"The judgment is now passing in the sanctuary above. For many years this work has been in progress. Soon—none know how soon—it will pass to the cases of the living."* When the Judgment passes to the living, the Final Events listed will begin from the left side of the chart and pass to the right side, culminating with the Second Coming of Christ.

The Judgment is described in *The Faith I Live By*, p. 212. *"As the books of record are opened in the judgment, the lives of all who have believed on Jesus come in review before God. Beginning with those who first lived upon the earth, our Advocate presents the cases of each successive generation, and closes with the living. Every name is mentioned, every case closely investigated. Names are accepted, names rejected. When any have sins remaining upon the books of record, unrepented of and unforgiven, their names will be blotted out of the book of life, and the record of their good deeds will be erased from the book of God's remembrance.*

All who have truly repented of sin, and by faith claimed the blood of Christ as their atoning sacrifice, have had pardon entered against their names in the books of heaven; as they have become partakers of the righteousness of Christ, and their characters are found to be in harmony with the law of God, their sins will be blotted out, and they themselves will be accounted worthy of eternal life." Through our advocate, Jesus, may each of us have this experience of being accounted worthy of eternal life!

When the Judgment of the Living begins, there is another Final Event that must begin with it if you are judged to be saved. This event is called the Sealing. Everyone who is judged to be saved has received the Seal of God! Therefore, when the Judgment of the Living begins, the Sealing must begin as well.

The first group of people to be sealed is called the 144,000. Who or what is this Seal of God and the group called the 144,000? To understand the Seal of God and the 144,000 we must first understand the Close of Probation.

The Final Events Leading to the Second Coming of Jesus

	JUDGMENT OF THE LIVING BEGINS	FIRST SUNDAY LAW	Little Time of Trouble	PROBATION CLOSES FOR ISRAEL	Great Time of Trouble	SECOND COMING OF CHRIST
Judgment of the Living			Judgment of the Living Continues			
Sealing of 144,000			Sealing Continues			
Latter Rain Begins			Latter Rain Continues			
			The Loud Cry Given			
Sunday Law Agitation			2nd Sunday Law		3rd Sunday Law	
The Shaking					Time of Jacob's Trouble	
Coming of Satan & his Evil Angels					Work of Satan & Evil Angels Intensifies	
					Holy Spirit Withdrawn	
					The Seven Last Plagues	
Close of Probation as a Process			Close of Probation as a Process Continues			
					Battle of Armageddon	

The Close of Probation

When considering the Close of Probation, it is clear from the Bible and from Spirit of Prophecy passages that there are two different kinds of probation closings as we approach the end of this world. To simplify our understanding, we will call them the Close of Probation as a Process and the Close of Probation as a Point in Time.[1] The Close of Probation as a Process begins when the Judgment of the Living begins. In *Selected Messages*, Book 1, p. 66, Ellen White makes the statement: *"Reference to our published works will show our belief that the living righteous will receive the seal of God prior to the close of probation"*. Now I must ask you two questions to clarify our understanding of the Close of Probation. When you receive the Seal of God is your destiny fixed? And, has your judgment taken place? Yes, of course! Each individual on this planet that is saved will be judged and will receive the Seal of God prior to the Close of Probation, according to the Spirit of Prophecy. The Close of Probation named in this passage, when everyone on planet earth has been judged, is known as the Close of Probation as a Point in Time. Therefore, from the time the Judgment of the Living begins, until the Close of Probation as a Point in Time, individuals who have been judged to be saved will have received the Seal of God. Their destiny is fixed, and their individual probation on planet earth has closed. Likewise, those who are judged to be lost will have received the Mark of the Beast; their destiny is fixed, and their individual probation is closed. This will occur for each individual at different time periods.

For example, for some, their individual close of probation will occur as the Judgment of the Living begins, while for others it will occur as the Agitation of the Sunday Law progresses. For others, it will take place at the beginning of the Little Time of Trouble, at the middle of the Little Time of Trouble, or at the last phases of the Little Time of Trouble. This is known as The Close of Probation as a Process.

When the time comes that every person on this planet has made a final decision for or against Jesus Christ, and therefore has been judged and received either the Seal of God or the Mark of the Beast, then the Close of Probation as a Point in Time occurs. It is at the Close of

Probation as a Point in Time that Jesus ceases His mediatorial ministry on our behalf and stands up in the heavenly sanctuary.

Daniel 12:1 begins by describing the Close of Probation as a Point in Time in this way, *"And at that time shall Michael stand up, the great prince which standeth for the children of thy people "*. Who is Michael, our great prince? He is Jesus, of course. Jesus, the One who stands for us in the judgment, stands up on the throne signifying the end of the Judgment of the Living and the commencement of the Close of Probation as a Point in Time.

Daniel continues, *"and there shall be a time of trouble, such as never was since there was a nation even to that same time: and at that time thy people shall be delivered, every one that shall be found written in the book."* Jesus stands up; the judgment has been concluded, the Close of Probation as a Point in Time has taken place, and we are thrown into *"a time of trouble, such as never was since there was a nation "*. This time of trouble is known as the Great Time of Trouble, seen on your chart extending from the third vertical line—when the Close of Probation as a Point in Time occurs—to the fourth vertical line when the Second Coming of Christ occurs, which is the time *"thy people shall be delivered "*. Thus, in Daniel 12:1 we see a description of the Great Time of Trouble.

At this juncture I want to clarify a point that many individuals misunderstand when studying the Final Events. At the time when Jesus stands up in the heavenly sanctuary and the judgment is finished, God does not say, "too bad if you're not ready and you haven't accepted Me, the judgment is over, it's too late, and it's your tough luck." Our God would never do such a thing! The Final Events will bring every person on this planet to a final decision for or against Jesus Christ. The Judgment of the Living is simply God's recognition of the final decision you and I have made—a decision that will be made based on the strength of our relationship with Jesus Christ!

We will see throughout our study of the Final Events that the necessary ingredient to see us through those events and carry us into the kingdom of heaven is a strong relationship with Jesus!

The Seal of God

Hitherto we have seen that when the Judgment of the Living begins, the Sealing begins. What is the Seal of God? Traditionally we have believed that the Seal of God is the Seventh-day Sabbath. More recently, though, in our publications and books a new idea has been introduced and promoted: the belief that the Seal of God is the Father's name written in the forehead or, in other words, the character of God written in the mind and heart.

What is the Seal of God, then? Is it the Seventh-day Sabbath, or the Father's name written in the forehead? Let's weigh the evidence to determine the answer to this question.

Revelation 7:2,3 states, *"And I saw another angel ascending from the east, having the seal of the living God: and he cried with a loud voice to the four angels, to whom it was given to hurt the earth and the sea, Saying, Hurt not the earth, neither the sea, nor the trees, till we have sealed the servants of our God in their foreheads."* Where is the Seal of God received? It is received in the forehead or, in other words, in the mind.

Revelation 14:1 says, *"And I looked, and, lo, a Lamb stood on the mount Sion, and with him an hundred forty and four thousand, having his Father's name written in their foreheads."* Obviously, as detailed in Scripture, the Seal of God is received in the forehead and the Father's name is received or written in the forehead as well. Some well-meaning Christians have assumed from these Scriptures that the Seal of God then is the Father's name written in the forehead. However, if I were to consider two separate beliefs, both of which I personally believe, wouldn't you say they were both written in my forehead? Does the fact that they are both located in my forehead make both of these sets of beliefs the same thing? Absolutely not! It does allow for the possibility of them being identical, but does not give us conclusive proof that this is so. They could be very different sets of beliefs!

Bible Commentary, Vol. 7, p. 981 states, *"There is to be a mark placed upon God's people, and that mark is the keeping of His holy Sabbath."* In this Spirit of Prophecy quotation we see that the mark that is placed upon God's people, which other passages tell us is called the Seal of God, is the keeping of His holy Sabbath.

In The Great Controversy, p. 640, the following statement is made: *"Too late they see that the Sabbath of the fourth commandment is the seal of the living God."* In this passage the Spirit of Prophecy declares that the Seal of God is the Seventh-day Sabbath. The question, then, is, where are we getting this idea that the Seal of God is the Father's name written in the forehead or God's character written in the mind and heart?

There are a few Spirit of Prophecy passages that seem to support this position. In the *Review and Herald,* June 10, 1902 is the following: *"Are we seeking for His fullness, ever pressing toward the mark set before us, the perfection of His character? When the Lord's people reach this mark, they will be sealed in their foreheads."*

The *Review and Herald,* May 21, 1895 says, *"The seal of the living God will be placed upon those only who bear a likeness to Christ in character."* Apparently, one of the conditions of receiving the Seal of God is to be Christ-like and have God's character in our forehead. These texts do not state explicitly, though, that the Seal of God is the character of God in our forehead or mind; only that having the character of God is a condition of receiving the Seal of God.

Testimonies, Vol. 5, p. 216 says, *"Now is the time to prepare. The seal of God will never be placed upon the forehead of an impure man or woman. It will never be placed upon the forehead of the ambitious, world-loving man or woman. It will never be placed upon the forehead of men or women of false tongues or deceitful hearts. All who receive the seal must be without spot before God—candidates for heaven."* Those who receive the Seal of God must have allowed Jesus to be Lord of their lives and allowed Him to change them to be like He is, to have His character. Jesus will change us through our relationship with Him. All we must do is allow Him to.

We have reviewed several texts that it seems could support either side of the question. The Spirit of Prophecy states in one particular passage that the Sabbath is the Seal of God. Revelation 14 and other Spirit of Prophecy passages seem to support the possibility that the Seal of God is the character of God or the Father's name written in our forehead.

In my personal study, as I pondered all of these texts while researching this subject, I came to the following quotation from the *Bible Commentary, EGW Comments,* p. 1161, which changed my perspective and understanding of the subject, and provided me the answer to the question of what the Seal of God is! *"Just as soon as the people of God are sealed in their foreheads—it is not any seal or mark that can be seen, but a settling into the truth, both intellectually and spiritually, so they cannot be moved—just as soon as God's people are sealed and prepared for the shaking, it will come."*

First of all, this passage identifies the time period when the Shaking will occur. It states that after God's people (the initial group called the 144,000) are sealed, the Shaking will occur. If you look at the chart on page 5 you will see that the Shaking occurs during the Little Time of Trouble, and the 144,000 are sealed by the time we reach the beginning of the Little Time of Trouble. You will see that much more clearly as we continue this study.

This passage also describes the Seal of God not as something that can be seen but as a settling into the truth both intellectually and spiritually so that you cannot be moved. What truth is being spoken of in this passage? Well, all born-again Christians have settled into the truth contained in nine of the Ten Commandments. Those nine commandments could not be the truth we need to settle into so that we cannot be moved as we approach the end of this world. However, the fourth commandment, the commandment to observe the Seventh-day Sabbath is the truth not being followed by many professed Christians. This is the truth all Christians must settle into. The Seal of God, then, is a settling into the Seventh-day Sabbath truth both intellectually and spiritually so that we cannot be moved as we approach the end of this world.

How do we settle into the Sabbath truth intellectually so that we cannot be moved? By accepting what the Lord has said in His fourth commandment concerning the Seventh-day Sabbath and being willing to follow that command no matter what! Those that settle into the Sabbath truth intellectually pass the Mark of the Beast test as we approach the end of this world.

How do we settle into the Sabbath truth spiritually so that we cannot be moved? Well, what does the Sabbath commandment state that we must do in a spiritual sense? We must keep the seventh day holy! By keeping the Seventh-day Sabbath holy we have settled into the Sabbath truth spiritually.

How do we keep the Seventh-day Sabbath holy? Are sinful people able to keep the Seventh-day Sabbath holy? The answer to these questions is found in *Desire of Ages*, p. 283: *"No other institution which was committed to the Jews tended so fully to distinguish them from surrounding nations as did the Sabbath. God designed that its observance should designate them as His worshipers. It was to be a token of their separation from idolatry, and their connection with the true God. But in order to keep the Sabbath holy, men must themselves be holy. Through faith they must become partakers of the righteousness of Christ."*

For each one of us to have the ability to follow the Seventh-day Sabbath spiritually by keeping it holy, we must have allowed Jesus to make us a holy person through our faith relationship with Him. Once we have become holy and therefore are able to keep the Seventh-day Sabbath holy, we are then able to obey all of the other commandments as well. This is why the Seventh-day Sabbath is the pinnacle of the Ten Commandments. This is why the Seventh-day Sabbath is the Seal of the living God. It is the last of the Ten Commandments that we will be able to observe. Once we are able to observe the Seventh-day Sabbath we have been made holy by the work of the Holy Spirit. We can now observe all of the Ten Commandments and are ready for heaven.

The Seventh-day Sabbath is the Seal of the living God. When you have a package and put a seal over it, the seal is the final item that is applied to complete the package. But is the seal the whole package? No, of course not! However, that is what those who claim that the Seal of God is the Father's name written in the forehead are saying. The Father's name, which is the character of God, is all of the Ten Commandments, the whole package. The Seal of the living God is the observance of the Seventh-day Sabbath by keeping it holy, the pinnacle of the Ten Commandments, and the last of the Ten Commandments we will be able to observe. The result of the Seal is the ability to follow all of the Ten Commandments and thus have the character of God, the Father's name written in our forehead. This understanding fits consistently with all of the passages listed above.

In *Letter 31, 1898,* Ellen White writes, *"The sign of obedience is the observance of the Sabbath of the fourth commandment. If men keep the fourth commandment, they will keep all the rest."* The Seventh-day

Sabbath is the last commandment we will finally be able to keep, the pinnacle of the Ten Commandments. Once we are able to observe the Seventh-day Sabbath commandment, we have been made holy, our character is complete, we have settled into the Seventh-day Sabbath truth spiritually, and as long as we have settled into the Sabbath truth intellectually, so that we cannot be moved, we have been sealed.

The Creation of Holiness

In the *Review and Herald*, Nov. 1, 1892, the Spirit of Prophecy says, *"Through faith the Holy Spirit works in the heart to create holiness therein; but this cannot be done unless the human agent will work with Christ. We can be fitted for heaven only through the work of the Holy Spirit upon the heart."* How do we work with Christ to allow the Holy Spirit to work upon our hearts? Through faith in Christ we must create an atmosphere in which the Holy Spirit can work. How do we do that? Well, let's take, for example, the television. If we watch television for six hours during the day, are we creating an atmosphere that can allow the Holy Spirit to work? We probably are not, unless we are watching Christian programming. On the other hand, if we spend an hour in God's Word in the morning and talk to Him throughout the day, looking for His leading in our lives, and pray to Him in the evening, are we creating an atmosphere in which the Holy Spirit can work? Yes, of course!

As we spend time in God's Word, the Holy Spirit works in a mighty way upon our minds and hearts as He takes those principles and instructions that Jesus gives us in His Word and places them in our hearts and minds. As we accept those principles and instructions in our hearts and minds we begin to follow them with the Holy Spirit's help and guidance.

In addition, as we talk to God in prayer throughout the day and look for His leading in our lives and experience that leading our faith increases, our trust in Him swells, and our relationship with Him grows much stronger. As we continue this relationship with God on a daily basis, allowing Him to talk to us through His Word (and in a sense through answered prayer), and talking back to Him in prayer, thereby focusing on Jesus and His presence throughout the day, this relationship development slowly creates holiness within us.

At this juncture the question many people ask is will we ever feel holy? No, I don't believe we will ever feel holy due to the fact Satan and his evil angels constantly remind us of our past.

When we think of our past failures, short-comings, and sins, it will be hard for us to finally believe we have arrived and now walk with Jesus in a sinless life. In fact, the closer we come to Jesus, the less we feel that way. Only Jesus will know when we have reached the point of true holiness.

To become a holy person our focus should not be on becoming holy. Our focus should be on our relationship with Jesus! He will make us the holy person He desires us to be.

As we approach the end of this world, the events that take place will lead us to a closer walk with our Lord than ever before. Through our close, daily relationship with Him we will be led by the Holy Spirit into complete holiness, and therefore will be able to keep the Seventh-day Sabbath holy, follow all of God's Ten Commandments, and accordingly will have received the Seal of God.

This is what heaven wants to do for us. However, we must allow it to happen. Satan and his evil angels are very crafty at keeping us from the Word of God and from the daily relationship our Lord wants so much to have with us, which will prepare us for heaven and these Final Events.

The late Joe Crews, the former speaker and director of the *Amazing Facts* television and radio program, once stated that at age sixteen he began to practice the presence of God in his life on a daily basis, so that everywhere he went he took the Lord with him. Friend, do you realize what that will do to your life? Try to sit down in front of the television with Jesus by your side and see what that does to your programming selections. With Jesus by your side, every aspect of your life will begin to change.

How Did Enoch Make it to Heaven?

In *Sermons and Talks*, Vol. 1, p. 2, the Spirit of Prophecy describes how Enoch was translated to heaven without seeing death. *"Enoch walked with God three hundred years previous to his translation to heaven, and the state of the world was not then more favorable for the perfection of Christian character than it is today. And how did Enoch walk with God? He educated his mind and heart to ever feel that he was in the presence of God, and when in perplexity his prayers would ascend to God to keep him.*

He refused to take any course that would offend his God. He kept the Lord continually before him. He would pray, "Teach me Thy way, that I may not err. What is Thy pleasure concerning me? What shall I do to honor Thee, my God?" Thus he was constantly shaping his way and course in accordance with God's commandments, and he had perfect confidence and trust in his heavenly Father, that He would help him. He had no thought or will of his own. It was all submerged in the will of his Father.

Now Enoch was a representative of those who will be upon the earth when Christ shall come, who will be translated to heaven without seeing death."

I encourage you to begin today to practice the presence of God in your life as Enoch did. Remember that at every step in your life Jesus is present with you. Talk to Him as you would to a friend. Allow Him to talk to you through His Word and answered prayer. He will change you to be like He is and prepare you for heaven.

The Daily Relationship with God Is Essential

Heaven must be our priority as we approach the end of this world. We must have that daily relationship with God. However, according to surveys, that is not the state of affairs among Seventh-day Adventist Christians. Surveys have indicated that a large percentage of Seventh-day Adventists do not have a daily relationship with Jesus Christ. They therefore are not allowing the changes to take place that heaven desires. They are not allowing the grace of God to do its work to change them to be like Jesus and prepare them for Jesus' Second Coming. This is the central theme of the Final Events. Jesus so earnestly desires us to spend the time with Him so that He can prepare us for the Final Events and for heaven.

Pastor/author Morris Venden once said that on one particular Sabbath he told his congregation that on the following day they should play golf utilizing their sledge hammer, by putting the sledge hammer through their television set. He then paused and allowed this statement to sink in. He then stepped up to the microphone and told his congregation that he wanted them to do this only under one condition. That condition was that if they found that they spent more time watching television each day than they spent in the Word of God, then they should take that sledge hammer and play golf with it, by putting the head of it through the television, and then framing the sledge hammer and hanging it on the wall. Why? Because that act may very well allow them to spend more time with Jesus on a daily basis, which will allow Jesus to make the changes required in them, and prepare them for the Final Events, and prepare them for heaven!

Prophets and Kings, p. 626 says, *"Christians should be preparing for what is soon to break upon the world as an overwhelming surprise. And this preparation they should make by diligently studying the Word of God and striving to conform their lives to its precepts."* Let's spend the time with Jesus in His Word on a daily basis, strive to be like He is, and practice His presence with us, which will facilitate our preparedness for His return!

The 144,000

Some of the characteristics of the 144,000 are given in Revelation 14:1-5: *"And I looked, and, lo, a Lamb stood on the mount Sion, and with him an hundred forty and four thousand, having his Father's name written in their foreheads."* The 144,000 have the character of God!

"And I heard a voice from heaven, as the voice of many waters, and as the voice of a great thunder: and I heard the voice of harpers harping with their harps: And they sung as it were a new song before the throne, and before the four beasts, and the elders: and no man could

learn that song but the hundred and forty and four thousand, which were redeemed from the earth. These are they which were not defiled with women; for they are virgins." What is a woman in symbolic Bible prophecy? A woman is a church. This text declares that the 144,000 have not been defiled by the false churches. What do the false churches do as we approach the end of this world? They break God's Ten Commandments, particularly the fourth. Apparently the 144,000, called virgins, is a group of people who have a pure faith and follow all of God's Ten Commandments. Obviously, then, the initial 144,000 will be made up of people who observe the Seventh-day Sabbath.

"These are they which follow the Lamb whithersoever he goeth. These were redeemed from among men, being the firstfruits unto God and to the Lamb." This initial group called the 144,000 is called the firstfruits. Why? These are the first people among the living that have been judged and received the Seal of God. They are the first ones to have been deemed to be saved, the first fruits.

Verse 5: *"And in their mouth was found no guile: for they are without fault before the throne of God."* These are a group of people who have maintained a close relationship with Jesus and allowed Him to change them to the point they can follow perfectly God's Ten Commandments as we approach the end of the world.

How does God change us, through our relationship with Him, to become part of this group called the 144,000? What part do we have in this process? The answer to these questions is found in the *Review and Herald,* March 19, 1889, Is It Well with My Soul? *"John saw a Lamb on Mount Zion, and with him 144,000, having his Father's name written in their foreheads. They bore the signet of heaven. They reflected the image of God. They were full of the light and the glory of the Holy One. If we would have the image and superscription of God upon us, we must separate ourselves from all iniquity. We must forsake every evil way, and then we must trust our cases in the hands of Christ. While we are working out our own salvation with fear and trembling, God will work in us to will and to do of his own good pleasure. While you must do your part, yet it is God that must give you aid, and sanctify you. Christ makes us penitent that he may forgive us. We have an idea that we must do some part of the work alone. We have thought that there are two or three steps that we must take without any help or support. But this is not so. The Spirit of God is continually wooing and drawing the soul to right purposes, and into harmony with the law of God."*

Immediately following this description of the 144,000 in Revelation 14 we find the Three Angels' Messages being declared. Most scholars then believe (which is supported by the Spirit of Prophecy) that this initial group called the 144,000 is the group that proclaims the Three Angels' Messages to the world via the Latter Rain in what is called the Loud Cry, which will be given during the Little Time of Trouble. In order to receive the Latter Rain and then give the Loud Cry during the Little Time of Trouble, this group must cleanse themselves from every defilement, through the work of the Holy Spirit in the Early Rain power, prior to the Little Time of Trouble.

This truth is revealed in *Testimonies*, Vol. 5, p. 214. *"Not one of us will ever receive the Seal of God while our characters have one spot or stain upon them. It is left with us to remedy the defects in our characters, to cleanse the soul temple of every defilement. Then the latter rain will fall upon us as the early rain fell upon the disciples on the Day of Pentecost."* We must first cleanse the soul temple of every defilement. Then the Latter Rain will be poured out upon us, which finishes God's work in us. We then have the character of God, are judged to be saved, receive the Seal of God, and give the Loud Cry during the Little Time of Trouble. Remember, the 144,000 have the character of God and the Seal of God.

This truth communicates a solemn warning to us not to wait until the Final Events arrive to develop our relationship with God and allow Him to change us to be like Jesus. We must allow Him to change us now so that we are prepared and ready when the Little Time of Trouble begins if we want to be part of the initial group called the 144,000. We will study this in great detail in chapter 3.

A further description of the 144,000 is given in Revelation 7:1-4. *"And after these things I saw four angels standing on the four corners of the earth, holding the four winds of the earth, that the wind should not blow on the earth, nor on the sea, nor on any tree. And I saw another angel ascending from the east, having the seal of the living God: and he cried with a loud voice to the four angels, to whom it was given to hurt the earth and the sea, Saying, Hurt not the earth, neither the sea, nor the trees, till we have sealed the servants of our God in their foreheads. And I heard the number of them which were sealed: and there were sealed an hundred and forty and four thousand of all the tribes of the children of Israel."* What are the winds in symbolic Bible prophecy? Winds are symbolic of strife, both political, with problems in the world, and physical, with great natural disasters that hurt the earth, the sea, and the trees. These winds are being held back to allow the 144,000 to be sealed.

Ellen White, in a sermon preached in the Seventh-day Adventist Church in Des Moines, Iowa, December 1, 1888 as recorded in *Sermons and Talks*, Vol. 1, pp 72, 73, described the experience of those who are striving to become part of the 144,000. *"When the world sees that we have an intensity of desire, some object that is out of sight, which by faith is to us a living reality, then it puts an incentive to investigate, and they see that there is certainly something worth having, for they see that this faith has made a wonderful change in our life and character.*

A transformation has taken place, and you are a different man. You are not the same passionate man that you used to be. You are not the same worldly man that you were. You are not the man that was giving way to lust and evil passions, evil surmisings, and evil speakings. You are not this man at all, because a transformation has taken place. What is it? The image of Christ reflected in you. Then you are bearing in view that there is a company to stand by and by on Mount Zion, and you want to be one of that company, and you are determined that you will form a part of that company. Let me read [Rev. 14:1-3 quoted.]

Why were they [the 144,000] so specially singled out? Because they had to stand with a wonderful truth right before the whole world, and receive their opposition, and while receiving this opposition they were to remember that they were sons and daughters of God, that they must have Christ formed within them the hope of glory. They were ever keeping in view the great and blessed hope that is before them. What is it? It is an eternal weight of glory. Nothing could surpass it."

The Group that No Man Could Number

It's interesting to note that in Revelation 7 there is also a second group. Verse 9 says, *"After this I beheld, and, lo, a great multitude, which no man could number, of all nations, and kindreds, and people, and tongues, stood before the throne, and before the Lamb, clothed with white robes, and palms in their hands".* This group is different than the 144,000. The 144,000 are from twelve tribes, 12,000 from each tribe of Israel. This is the true church of God, Spiritual Israel, the 144,000. However, we now have a second group, and they're from where? They are from all nations and kindreds and people and tongues. This is a much larger group than the 144,000.

"And cried with a loud voice, saying, Salvation to our God which sitteth upon the throne, and unto the Lamb. And all the angels stood round about the throne, and about the elders and the four beasts, and fell before the throne on their faces, and worshipped God, Saying, Amen: Blessing, and glory, and wisdom, and thanksgiving, and honour, and power, and might, be unto our God for ever and ever. Amen. And one of the elders answered, saying unto me, What are these which are arrayed in white robes? and whence came they? And I said unto him, Sir, thou knowest. And he said to me, These are they which came out of great tribulation, and have washed their robes, and made them white in the blood of the Lamb" (v. 10-14).

This second group passes through great tribulation. Obviously, they trek through the Little Time of Trouble and the Great Time of Trouble. During the Little Time of Trouble, this second group, who hears the Loud Cry from the 144,000, joins them, and they begin to share the Third Angel's Message as well. .

We have thus far determined that there is a group called the 144,000 that receives the Latter Rain, is judged, and sealed, by the time we get to the beginning of the crisis called the Little Time of Trouble. This group proclaims the Third Angel's Message during the Little Time of Trouble and a larger group, a group the Bible says no man can number, comes out of Babylon, the false churches, and out of all the other religions and tongues and people, to join the 144,000. They also receive the Latter Rain, are judged, and receive the Seal of God. Everyone on earth who is saved must be judged and sealed before the four winds are released to begin the Great Time of Trouble, when the Close of Probation as a Point in Time occurs.

The interesting thing to note is that the Spirit of Prophecy calls the group that is saved out of the Great Time of Trouble the 144,000. To understand this we will examine a passage from The Great Controversy, pp. 648, 649, that describes the 144,000 after being saved out of the Great Time of Trouble. *"Upon the crystal sea before the throne, that sea of glass as it were mingled with fire,—so resplendent is it with the glory of God,—are gathered the company that have 'gotten the victory over the beast, and over his image, and over his mark, and over the number of his name.' With the Lamb upon Mount Zion, "having the harps of God," they stand, the hundred and forty and four thousand that were redeemed from among men; and there is heard, as the sound of many waters, and as the sound of a great thunder, 'the voice of harpers harping with their harps.'"*

This group consists of both of the groups of Revelation 7, the 144,000 that give the Loud Cry and the group that responds to the Loud Cry that no man can number. All of them have gotten the victory over the beast and his image, etc. This will be seen more clearly later on in this passage.

"And they sing 'a new song' before the throne, a song which no man can learn save the hundred and forty and four thousand. It is the song of Moses and the Lamb—a song of deliverance. None but the hundred and forty-four thousand can learn that song; for it is the song of their experience—an experience such as no other company have ever had. 'These are they which follow the Lamb withersoever He goeth.' These, having been translated from the earth, from among the living, are counted as 'the first fruits unto God and to the Lamb.' Revelation 15:2,3;14:1-5."

Again, this group called the 144,000 comprises the people who have been translated from the earth among the living. In the context in which it is written, this includes all of the living saints, which would include both groups of Revelation 7.

'"These are they which came out of great tribulation;' they have passed through the time of trouble such as never was since there was a nation; they have endured the anguish of the time of Jacob's trouble; they have stood without an intercessor through the final outpouring of God's judgments. But they have been delivered, for they have 'washed their robes, and made them white in the blood of the Lamb.'"

This passage contains a direct quotation from Revelation 7:14, which describes the second group of Revelation 7, the one that no man could number. ("These are they which came out of great tribulation, and have washed their robes, and made them white in the blood of the Lamb.") This text reveals that the second group of Revelation 7 is part of the first group, the 144,000, at the Second Coming of Christ. The two groups are integrated and called the 144,000.

Also, those who endure the Time of Jacob's Trouble and pass through the Great Time of Trouble without an intercessor, are all those among the living who are saved, members of both groups of Revelation 7, not just the ones who initially give the Loud Cry. This will be seen more clearly as we study the Time of Jacob's Trouble in chapter 5.

What does that tell us? This is compelling evidence that the final 144,000 at the Second Coming of Christ consists of both groups in Revelation 7. The number 144,000 must then be symbolic. It cannot be a literal number. You can't start with a group called the 144,000 that gives the Loud Cry and, as millions join it, still call the group the 144,000 at the Second Coming of Christ if it is a literal number. It seems to me that the term 144,000 must be symbolic of God's true church, Spiritual Israel, His perfected church, thus the use of the number 12 in the description of this church.

In addition, the term 144,000 could not be literal because the Bible describes this group as comprising twelve thousand from each of the twelve tribes of Israel. In this day and age, other than Judah, the tribes of Israel have been scattered throughout the world and have intermingled with many other peoples and can no longer be distinguished. Those tribes no longer exist.

In Bible prophecy, how do we treat entities that do not exist? For example, the seven-headed beast with ten horns in the book of Revelation, how is it dealt with? It is treated as symbolic! We must also, then, treat the 144,000 as symbolic. The 144,000 are symbolic of God's true people, His perfected church, Spiritual Israel!

Friend, let me interpose here that whether you believe the 144,000 are symbolic or literal is of no consequence. The important factor is whether or not you and I become part of the 144,000, obtain the character of God, and receive His seal.

In summary, the original 144000 are judged and sealed by the time we reach the beginning of the Little Time of Trouble. During the Little Time of Trouble the original 144,000, who have not been defiled by the Whore Babylon, give the Loud Cry, and a great multitude of people come out of all nations and tongues and people to join the 144,000. Many of these people were in false Christian churches and were keeping nine of the Ten Commandments. They were allowing the Holy Spirit to make them holy people. They were like the original 144,000. They spent the time with Jesus and had a deep abiding relationship with Him. They are Sunday keepers today and are becoming holy people, but they do not yet have an understanding of the Seventh-day Sabbath.

However, when the Loud Cry is given, they accept and begin to follow the Seventh-day Sabbath and keep it holy; their character is then complete, they receive the Seal of the living God, and they are saved as well. This is why in the chart on page 5 under the Little Time of Trouble you will see the phrase "sealing continues". The 144,000 are sealed initially. But then, during the Little Time of Trouble, the sealing continues as the great multitude of people that no man can number, who are called out of the world and out of Babylon, the false churches, and into the true church, join the true church, which is symbolized by the term "the 144,000." They have settled into the Sabbath truth, are keeping the Seventh-day Sabbath holy, are judged to be saved, and have received the Seal of God. Everyone must receive the Seal of God before the winds are released to start the Great Time of Trouble, when probation will be closed.

Now Is the Time of Salvation for Seventh-day Adventists

In *Testimonies,* Vol. 9, p. 97, the Spirit of Prophecy states, *"The time of God's destructive judgments is the time of mercy for those who have had no opportunity to learn what is truth. Tenderly will the Lord look upon them. His heart of mercy is touched; His hand is still stretched out to save, while the door is closed to those who would not enter."* The time of God's destructive judgments mentioned in this passage occurs during the Little Time of Trouble, as will be seen clearly in the next chapter. As we enter the Little Time of Trouble and God's destructive judgments fall, the door of salvation is open to those who have not had opportunity to learn the truth. However, the Lord's servant says that for those who have learned the truth but have not entered into that close relationship with Jesus, the door is closed. They will be shaken out of the church, as will be seen in Chapter 4. Now is the time of probation for all Seventh-day Adventists who have learned the truth. We must enter into a saved, close relationship with Jesus now! It will be too late once we enter the Little Time of Trouble. The message will then go to the rest of the world. No one who has learned the truth and professed to believe it can wait until the last moments of earth's history to build a close relationship with Jesus and follow Him. We must develop a close relationship with Jesus now and allow Him to prepare us for the Final Events before the crisis begins.

Let me interject here that all of us have loved ones and friends who may have heard the truth, especially our children, but are not following the truth and are not in the church at this time. I believe that as the Loud Cry is given, many of these will come back into the fold. The passage above that says that for certain individuals it is too late I believe refers to those that are currently in the church but have refused to enter into a close relationship with Jesus, and allow Him to change them to be like He is.

The Spirit of Prophecy states in the *Review and Herald*, Dec.13, 1892, *"And as we near the close of this earth's history, we either rapidly advance in Christian growth, or we rapidly retrograde toward the world."* We will go in either one direction or the other.

Remember the Parable of the Ten Virgins? There were five foolish virgins and five wise ones. Who are the virgins? We previously learned they are those who have not been defiled by the Whore Babylon (the false churches), have a pure faith, and keep all of God's Ten Commandments including the Seventh-day Sabbath. I believe that the Parable of the Ten Virgins applies more to Seventh-day Adventists than to any other group of Christians. We are called the virgins because we follow all of the Ten Commandments.

The Parable of the Ten Virgins says of the foolish virgins, *"Afterward came also the other virgins, saying, Lord, Lord, open to us. But he answered and said, Verily I say unto you, I know you not"* (Matt.

25:11, 12). The foolish virgins did not know Jesus. They were in the church. They acted like they were Christians. They claimed to follow all of the Ten Commandments. However, they did not know Jesus. What does that tell us today? We must spend time with Jesus. We must develop a strong relationship with Him. We can't afford to spend time with the television, playing golf, or being involved in any other recreation if that recreation takes too much time away from our relationship with Jesus. We must spend time with Him and allow Him to change us and prepare us for heaven, or we will not be ready for the Second Coming of Christ. We will be one of the foolish virgins.

In *Testimonies to Ministers and Gospel Workers*, p. 445, is the following: *"Those that overcome the world, the flesh, and the devil, will be the favored ones who shall receive the seal of the living God. Those whose hands are not clean, whose hearts are not pure, will not have the seal of the living God. Those who are planning sin and acting it will be passed by. Only those who, in their attitude before God, are filling the position of those who are repenting and confessing their sins in the great anti-typical day of atonement, will be recognized and marked as worthy of God's protection. The names of those who are steadfastly looking and waiting and watching for the appearing of their Saviour— more earnestly and wishfully than they who wait for the morning—will be numbered with those who are sealed. Those who, while having all the light of truth flashing upon their souls, should have works corresponding to their avowed faith, but are allured by sin, setting up idols in their hearts, corrupting their souls before God, and polluting those who unite with them in sin, will have their names blotted out of the book of life, and be left in midnight darkness, having no oil in their vessels with their lamps."* They did not have the Holy Spirit in their lives enough to create the new person Jesus so earnestly wants to change each one of us into and prepare us for the end of the world.

As I close this chapter there is only one question each of us must ask himself or herself individually as we approach the end of this world. Are the things you do each day helping you to settle into the truth? If so, then you are among the wise virgins. However, if the things you do every day are helping you to settle into the world, you will be among the foolish virgins; you will not be ready for the Second

Coming of Christ, and you will lose your eternal life. Jesus wants each one of us to come closer to Him with each passing day, to allow the Holy Spirit to change us and prepare us for heaven. Won't you, friend, accept the invitation of Jesus, and allow Him into your heart on a daily, moment-by-moment basis?

Chapter 2

The National Sunday Law & the Beginning of the Little Time of Trouble

Much has been said over the years concerning the National Sunday Law. The question that lingers is, what will this law do? A comment made in the *Seventh Bible Commentary*, p. 910, gives us an idea of how the National Sunday Law will occur and what transpires as a result: *"Protestantism shall give the hand of fellowship to the Roman power. Then there will be a law against the Sabbath of God's creation, and then it is that God will do His 'strange work' in the earth."* Notice that the Spirit of Prophecy reveals to us the fact that God will do a strange work in the earth as soon as a law is enacted that is against God's Sabbath and promotes Sunday. This strange work will be for the Creator to begin to destroy His own creation. Great natural disasters will begin to occur, especially in the larger cities. The National Sunday Law will, in effect, throw us into the Little Time of Trouble, as will be substantiated further over the course of this chapter and the two chapters that follow.

We gain more insight into this National Sunday Law from a Spirit of Prophecy passage found in the *Review and Herald*, Dec.18, 1888. *"A time is coming when the law of God is, in a special sense, to be made void in our land. The rulers of our nation will, by legislative enactments, enforce the Sunday law, and thus God's people be brought into great peril. When our nation, in its legislative councils, shall enact laws to bind the consciences of men in regard to their religious privileges, enforcing Sunday observance, and bringing oppressive power to bear against those who keep the seventh-day Sabbath, the law of God will, to all intents and purposes, be made void in our land; and national apostasy will be followed by national ruin."* This national apostasy that exalts the Sunday as God's Sabbath and degrades the Seventh-day Sabbath and those who follow it is called in Matthew 24 the "abomination that causes desolation" (NIV). When this apostasy occurs, God will do His strange work in the earth. Great natural disasters will take place. Economic ruin will occur. We have then been hurled into the Little Time of Trouble.

What will this Sunday law be like? America's first Sunday law was enacted in the Virginia colony in the year 1610. This law reads as follows: *"Every man and woman shall repair in the morning to the divine service and sermons preached upon the Sabbath day, and in the afternoon to divine service, and catechizing, upon pain for the first fault to lose their provision and the allowance for the whole week following; for the second, to lose the said allowance and also be whipt; and for the third to suffer death."*[2] That was the first Sunday law, and it almost parallels the three Sunday laws that will be enacted as we approach the end of the world.

Sunday blue laws have been established in each state and have existed in each state for a long time. During the 1880s and 1890s all forty-eight states had the Sunday laws. Seventeen of those forty-eight were using them to prosecute Sabbath keepers. In 1895 and 1896 there were seventy-six Seventh-day Adventists prosecuted in the United States and Canada. Twenty-eight served terms of various lengths in jails and on chain gangs for an aggregate total of 1144 days.[3]

The National Sunday Law of the 1880s

In 1888 and 1889 national Sunday laws came to the forefront through a man by the name of Wilbur Crafts, who, in 1880, became the pastor of a Congregationalist church in Brooklyn, New York. In an article in *Church History*, Gaines M. Foster writes about Crafts after he became a pastor. *"Three years later, Crafts published, under the title Successful Men Of To-day, a series of addresses he had delivered to young men in his church. . . . Not long after the publication of Successful Men Of To-day, which sold more than 40,000 copies, Crafts moved to a Presbyterian Church in New York City. There he preached a series of sermons on keeping the Sabbath. He first published them in 1884 as The Sabbath For Man and later expanded the book, which appeared in seven editions. Especially in its later editions, it compiled a great deal of information on the observance of the Sabbath, but the book consisted primarily of Crafts's warning that the Sabbath was imperiled. The threat, he maintained, came from Roman Catholic immigrants who had introduced in America the less-strict observance of the Sabbath that had appalled him in Europe. Crafts cited other dangers, including commercial amusements that opened on Sunday. The greatest threat, he thought, came from the national habit of treating the laws as a bill of fare, from which each one can take what he pleases. Crafts therefore demanded stricter enforcement of existing laws and called for new ones.*

Effective Sunday laws, Crafts argued, did not violate the separation of church and state because they did not impose religion. His claim rested on a distinction he drew between a religious Sabbath and a civil Sabbath. A civil Sabbath stopped all work on Sunday, not to foster religion, Crafts explained, but to promote public health and education, reduce crime, and preserve home and nation. In other places in the book, though, Crafts made it clear that he sought Sabbath laws for religious reasons. Sunday laws, he wrote, were necessary for the preservation of religion, and religion was necessary for the preservation of the state. The State, therefore, has a right to protect the morals of the community. Exercising its right over public morals did not, in Crafts's view, necessarily involve restrictions on liberty, unless liberty was defined as the freedom to do as one pleased.

The year after Sabbath for Man first appeared, Crafts began a campaign for a national Sunday law. He drew up a petition that asked Congress to ban military parades, mail, and interstate trains on Sunday and, for good measure, to establish a comprehensive Sunday law for the territories. In circulating his petition, Crafts received assistance from Josephine C. Bateham, head of the department on Sabbath observance of the Woman's Christian Temperance Union (WCTU) and from other Sabbath societies. As the petitions arrived in Congress in 1888, Henry W. Blair, a Senator from New Hampshire who was an ally of the WCTU, held a hearing on the issue before the Committee on Education and Labor, which he chaired. Crafts took charge of presenting the witnesses and also spoke. At the end of the hearing Blair announced that Congress had received nearly 21,000 petitions but as yet no one had introduced any legislation. At the Sabbath forces request, Blair prepared a sweeping bill that incorporated the provisions of Crafts's petition. In the territories, District of Columbia, and all other places under the exclusive jurisdiction of the United States, it banned all Sunday work, save that of necessity, and mercy and humanity, and all plays, games, or amusements that would disturb others. Blair's bill also outlawed, with some exceptions, Sunday mails, military and naval drills and parades, and much interstate commerce.

At Blair's suggestion, Crafts presented the bill to the Knights of Labor and other unions, and they endorsed it. The WCTU, along with the various Sabbath associations, circulated petitions in its behalf. Crafts, however, decided that the campaign demanded a new organization. In the spring of 1888, he convinced the Methodist Episcopal Church to create a committee on Sabbath reform and to invite other denominations to join in working for proper observance of the Sabbath. The main northern and southern Presbyterian churches, the American Baptist Home Mission Society, the Congregationalists, and other denominations agreed to participate. Later that year, the group formally organized as the American Sabbath Union (ASU). Elliot F. Shepard became the President and Crafts, who resigned his pastorate, its Field Secretary.

During that meeting in December of 1888, Blair's committee held a second hearing on the bill for a national Sunday law. Crafts, Bateham of the WCTU, and others spoke in its behalf, but many opponents, including religious liberals and Seventh Day Adventists, testified against it. After the hearings, Crafts traveled the country mobilizing support. Even though Blair's committee received many petitions in favor of the bill, it failed to report it. Sabbath forces still claimed a partial victory since the Post Office reduced its activities on Sunday, and the army moved its formal inspections from Sunday to Saturday."[4]

This bill for a national Sunday law was defeated, but I believe the law came to the forefront at this time to help Ellen White better understand, through visions given by God, the final National Sunday Law that will be in place as we approach the end of the world. She has used this understanding given her from heaven to counsel us concerning this final event.

The National Sunday Law Today

The question we must ask ourselves today is, are we headed toward national Sunday laws? Since 1994, the ecumenical movement has grown substantially and was originally promoted by organizations such as The Christian Coalition and the Catholic Alliance. The plan of those groups was to unite Christianity on common points of doctrine. The most common point of doctrine, of course, is the observance of Sunday as the Sabbath.

Well, during the 1990s, that goal was never achieved. However, there are new organizations taking the place of the older ones, with similar goals, such as Christian Churches Together and the Faith and Values Coalition, a resurrection of the 1980s organization called the Moral Majority. These are active organizations that in various ways promote the ecumenical movement.

The Great Controversy, p. 445, says, *"When the leading churches of the United States, uniting upon such points of doctrine as are held by them in common, shall influence the state to enforce their decrees and to sustain their institutions, then Protestant America will have formed an image of the Roman hierarchy, and the infliction of civil penalties upon dissenters will inevitably result."* Since the 1990s, a movement to unite all of Christianity on common points of doctrine has been gaining stride and continues to expand to this day!

During the time the National Sunday Law was promoted in late 1888 and early 1889, Ellen White, in the *Review and Herald*, Jan.1, 1889, said, *"Prophecy represents Protestantism as having lamb-like horns, but speaking like a dragon. Already we are beginning to hear the voice of the dragon. There is a satanic force propelling the Sunday movement, but it is concealed. Even the men who are engaged in the*

work, are themselves blinded to the results which will follow their move-
ment. Let not the commandment-keeping people of God be silent at
this time, as though we gracefully accepted the situation. There is the
prospect before us, of waging a continuous war, at the risk of imprison-
ment, of losing property and even life itself, to defend the law of God,
which is being made void by the laws of men. This Bible text will be
quoted to us, 'Let every soul be subject unto the higher powers. . . . The
powers that be are ordained of God'."

The Final National Sunday Law

When the powers that be, who are the majority, try to initiate the Sunday law, they will point to this biblical text in claiming themselves to be the higher powers that are ordained of God. They will criticize harshly those who oppose them, and promote the observance of God's Seventh-day Sabbath. We are counseled at this time not to be silent but to stand up for the law of God. Seventh-day Adventists stood up for the law of God in 1888, 1889 and the Sunday law was defeated at that time. We must stand up for the law of God as we approach the end of this world, even in the face of fierce persecution, to keep the Sunday law at bay as long as possible. In this Sunday Law Agitation time period the church will awaken from its sleeping, Laodicean condition, and indi- viduals will develop their relationship with Jesus to such a degree that they will receive the Latter Rain as well as the Seal of God. They had been broadcasting the Three Angels' Messages, but now do so with power as will be seen in the next chapter.

The Bible gives us a picture of the action to be taken by God's Ten Commandment-keeping Christians once the National Sunday Law is enacted. *"When ye therefore shall see the abomination of desolation [the NIV says "the abomination that causes desolation"], spoken of by Daniel the prophet, stand in the holy place, (whoso readeth, let him un- derstand:) Then let them which be in Judaea flee into the mountains: Let him which is on the housetop not come down to take any thing out of his house: Neither let him which is in the field return back to take his clothes. And woe unto them that are with child, and to them that give suck in those days! But pray ye that your flight be not in the winter, nei- ther on the sabbath day: For then shall be great tribulation, such as was not since the beginning of the world to this time, no, nor ever shall be* (Matt. 24:15-21). As stated earlier, the abomination that causes desolation is the enactment of the National Sunday Law, which will throw us into the Little Time of Trouble as the Lord responds to this abomination with great natural disasters. The Bible tells us to flee to the mountains at this time.

The Spirit of Prophecy expands on this biblical passage in *Testimonies* Vol. 5, pp. 464, 465. *"As the siege of Jerusalem by the Roman armies was the signal for flight to the Judean Christians, so the assumption of power on the part of our nation in the decree enforcing the papal sabbath will be a warning to us. It will then be time to leave the large cities, preparatory to leaving the smaller ones for retired homes in secluded places among the mountains."* We are instructed to leave the larger cities and eventually the smaller cities when the National Sunday Law is passed, to avoid the persecution that will come to those who follow God's Ten Commandments and to avoid the wrath of God which will be poured out on the larger cities (as will be revealed in the following paragraphs and in chapter 4).

We have further instruction on how to handle this National Sunday Law in *Testimonies*, Vol. 9, pp.232, 233. *"To defy the Sunday laws will but strengthen in their persecution the religious zealots who are seeking to enforce them. Give them no occasion to call you law breakers . . . One does not receive the mark of the beast because he shows that he realizes the wisdom of keeping the peace by refraining from work that gives offence"*. Ellen White clearly tells us here not to defy the Sunday laws. We are counseled to keep the peace by going along with the authorities and refraining from work on Sundays. We do not receive the Mark of the Beast by following this law. We are to continue to follow God's Ten Commandments by promoting and worshipping on and keeping as our Sabbath the Seventh-day Sabbath. The Mark of the Beast is given to those who promote and insist on worshipping on and keeping as their Sabbath the Venerable Day of the Sun without regard to God's Ten Commandments.

The Spirit of Prophecy continues with further counsel as to what to do on Sundays, as follows: *"Sunday can be used for carrying forward various lines of work that will accomplish much for the Lord. On this day open-air meetings and cottage meetings can be held. House-to-*

house work can be done. Those who write can devote this day to writing their articles. Whenever it is possible, let religious services be held on Sunday. Make these meetings intensely interesting. Sing genuine revival hymns, and speak with power and assurance of the Saviour's love."

The Spirit of Prophecy further expands our understanding of this time period in *Testimonies for the Church*, Vol. 5, p. 451. *"By the decree enforcing the institution of the papacy in violation of the law of God, our nation will disconnect herself fully from righteousness. . . . As the approach of the Roman armies was a sign to the disciples of the impending destruction of Jerusalem, so may this apostasy be a sign to us that the limit of God's forbearance is reached, that the measure of our nation's iniquity is full, and that the angel of mercy is about to take her flight, never to return."* Again, this is when we are thrust into the Little Time of Trouble as God responds to the National Sunday Law with great natural disasters that begin to occur in the United States.

This principle is further expanded in the *Review and Herald*, June 15, 1897. *"Protestants will work upon the rulers of the land to make laws to restore the lost ascendancy of the man of sin, who sits in the temple of God, showing himself that he is God. Roman Catholic principles will be taken under the care and protection of the state. This national apostasy will speedily be followed by national ruin. The protest of Bible truth will be no longer tolerated by those who have not made the law of God their rule of life. Then will the voice be heard from the graves of martyrs, represented by the souls that John saw slain for the word of God and the testimony of Jesus Christ which they held."* Evidently, when the National Sunday Law is legislated and the Little Time of Trouble begins, there will be martyrs from among those who follow God's Ten Commandments.

Testimonies for the Church, Vol. 6, p.396, states, *"Foreign nations will follow the example of the United States. Though she leads out, yet the same crisis will come upon our people in all parts of the world."* Sunday laws will then be enacted throughout the world as Protestantism combines church with state worldwide. (A further understanding of this principle, which concerns the seven heads of Revelation 17, may be found in my book *The Final Catastrophic Events*). This results in a worldwide persecution of God's true people, those who follow all of His Ten Commandments.

A glimpse of this persecution is depicted in *Selected Messages*, Book 3, p. 397. *"The two armies will stand distinct and separate, and this distinction will be so marked that many who shall be convinced of the truth will come on the side of God's commandment-keeping people. When this grand work is to take place in the battle* [during the Little Time of Trouble], *prior to the last closing conflict* [which will take place during the Great Time of Trouble, the Battle of Armageddon], *many will be imprisoned, many will flee for their lives from cities and towns, and many will be martyrs for Christ's sake in standing in defense of the truth."*

The *Review and Herald*, Apr.15, 1884, gives us a glimpse of what prison will be like: *"Our enemies will thrust us into prisons, but prison walls cannot cut off the communication between Christ and our souls. One who sees our every weakness, who is acquainted with every trial, is above all earthly powers; and angels can come to us in lonely cells, bringing light and peace from Heaven. The prison will be as a palace, for the rich in faith dwell there; and the gloomy walls will be lighted up with heavenly light"*. What a blessing that will be! We must remember that during this time of persecution, whether we are in prisons or fleeing for our lives to the mountains, Jesus and His angels will be with us.

Should we worry about this time of trouble? The Spirit of Prophecy gives us the answer to that question in *Manuscript Release*, Vol. 2, p. 329. *"As we approach the end of the earth's history we shall have increased power, proportionate to the trials to which we are subjected. We are not to keep ourselves in a state of worry and doubt, binding up our souls in the perplexities of unbelief and worldliness, in worrying and scolding and fretting, but wait on the Lord, in perfect obedience to His will, and we shall see the salvation of God from day to day. He always gives strength as our day shall be—strength and grace proportionate to the trials and tests and conflicts we are obliged to meet."* This is a moment in time when we must have come to the place where we trust the Lord implicitly to see us through this time of trouble. He will give us the additional strength and power just when we need it!

We will conclude this chapter on the National Sunday Law and the beginning of the Little Time of Trouble with a quotation from the Spirit of Prophecy in *The Upward Look*, p. 82. *"The Lord has not concealed from His followers the plan of the battle. He has presented before His people the great conflict, and He has given them words of encouragement. He charges them not to enter into the battle without counting the cost, while He assures them that they do not fight alone, but that supernatural agencies will enable the weak, if they trust in Him, to become strong against the vast confederacy of evil arrayed against them. He points them to the universe of heaven, and assures them that holy beings are wrestling against principalities and powers and the rulers of the darkness of this world, and against spiritual wickedness in high places. The children of God are cooperating with all the invisible host of light. And more than angels are in their ranks; the Holy Spirit, the representative of the Captain of the Lord's host, comes down to direct the battle."* Amen.

Chapter 3

The Little Time of Trouble: the Latter Rain, the Counsel of the True Witness, and the Loud Cry

After the National Sunday Law is enacted and we are thrust into the Little Time of Trouble, several events will take place. One of these events that will manifest itself in a mighty way during the Little Time of Trouble and actually begins just prior to the Little Time of Trouble is the Latter Rain. The Bible makes a statement concerning the Latter Rain as follows: *"And it shall come to pass in the last days, saith God, I will pour out of my Spirit upon all flesh: and your sons and your daughters shall prophesy, and your young men shall see visions, and your old men shall dream dreams: And on my servants and on my handmaidens I will pour out in those days of my Spirit; and they shall prophesy"* (Acts 2:17,18). The Latter Rain, of course, is the outpouring of the Holy Spirit as we approach the end of this world.

In *Testimonies to Ministers and Gospel Workers*, p. 506, the Spirit of Prophecy states, *"As the dew and the rain are given first to cause the seed to germinate, and then to ripen the harvest, so the Holy Spirit is given to carry forward, from one stage to another, the process of spiritual growth. The ripening of the grain represents the completion of the work of God's grace in the soul. By the power of the Holy Spirit the moral image of God is to be perfected in the character. We are to be wholly transformed into the likeness of Christ."* In this statement, the rain that germinates the seed and ripens the harvest is said to be the work of the Holy Spirit in the process of spiritual growth. The Holy Spirit is the One who transforms us to be the holy person Jesus wants us to be.

The apostle Peter gives us an understanding of the time period when the Latter Rain will fall. *"Repent ye therefore, and be converted, that your sins may be blotted out, when the times of refreshing shall come from the presence of the Lord; And he shall send Jesus Christ, which before was preached unto you" (Acts 3:19, 20).* As we examine these verses we must ask ourselves the question, when are our sins blotted out? They are officially blotted out in the judgment. According to these Bible verses then, when the times of refreshing come, the Judgment of the Living begins, followed by the Second Coming of Christ. What is the time of refreshing known as? It is known as the Latter Rain, as you will see in subsequent passages. Apparently, when the Latter Rain begins the Judgment of the Living begins as well. You will see this outlined in the chart on page 5.

Will we receive the Latter Rain if we have not received the Early Rain? *Testimonies to Ministers and Gospel Workers*, p. 506, explains. *"The latter rain, ripening earth's harvest, represents the spiritual grace that prepares the church for the coming of the Son of man. But unless the former rain has fallen, there will be no life; the green blade will not spring up. Unless the early showers have done their work, the latter rain can bring no seed to perfection."* Obviously, if the Early Rain hasn't done its work, to bring us to the point where Jesus is our Lord and He has been able to change us to be like He is, then the Latter Rain will not be able to do its work in bringing us to perfection.

Let us pinpoint the time when the Latter Rain will do its most extensive work. *Early Writings*, pp. 85, 86 states, *"The commencement of that time of trouble, here mentioned does not refer to the time when the plagues shall begin to be poured out* [the Great Time of Trouble], *but to a short period just before they are poured out, while Christ is in the sanctuary. At that time, while the work of salvation is closing, trouble will be coming on the earth, and the nations will be angry, yet held in check so as not to prevent the work of the third angel. At that time the "latter rain", or refreshing from the presence of the Lord, will come, to*

*give power to the loud voice of the third angel, and prepare the saints
to stand in the period when the seven last plagues shall be poured out."*
This short period, a time of trouble before the plagues will be poured
out, is known as the Little Time of Trouble. We previously learned that
the 144,000 receive the Latter Rain, are judged, and sealed by the time
we reach the beginning of the Little Time of Trouble. They then give
the Loud Cry during the Little Time of Trouble.

We also learned that as the Latter Rain falls the Judgment of the
Living begins. Since the 144,000 receive the Latter Rain (which com-
pletes their character), are judged, and sealed by the time we reach the
beginning of the Little Time of Trouble, one could assume the Latter
Rain will begin just prior to the Little Time of Trouble, progress as the
National Sunday Law is being agitated, and will be poured out most extensively once the National Sunday Law is enacted, during the Little
Time of Trouble, when probation is still open, since Christ is still in the
sanctuary.

Why is the Latter Rain given to God's people? The Spirit of
Prophecy declares that it comes for two reasons. First, the Latter Rain
comes to give power to the Loud Cry of the Third Angel's Message. It
comes to help God's people, the 144,000, to alert the world to the impending coming of Jesus Christ and warn it to come out of Babylon,
the false churches, which have insisted on the observance of the
Venerable Day of the Sun. It helps God's people to implore the world,
in the face of major persecution, to completely follow Jesus Christ and
all of His Ten Commandments.

Second, it prepares God's people to stand when the Seven Last
Plagues will be poured out as it brings God's people to perfection. This
time period when the Seven Last Plagues are poured out is known as the
Great Time of Trouble, when probation is closed (Chapters 5 and 6).

The Latter Rain will finish God's work in us. However, in order to
receive the Latter Rain, we must be developing a strong relationship
with Jesus now on a daily basis, to allow the Early Rain to do its work
and prepare us for the time of the Latter Rain.

This truth can be better understood by comparing the physical and
the spiritual application of the Latter Rain. A description of the physical Latter Rain is found in Deuteronomy 11:13-17. *"And it shall come*

to pass, if ye shall hearken diligently unto my commandments which I command you this day, to love the LORD your God, and to serve him with all your heart and with all your soul, That I will give you the rain of your land in his due season, the first rain and the latter rain, that thou mayest gather in thy corn, and thy wine, and thine oil. And I will send grass in thy fields for thy cattle, that thou mayest eat and be full. Take heed to yourselves, that your heart be not deceived, and ye turn aside, and serve other gods, and worship them; And then the Lord's wrath be kindled against you, and he shut up the heaven, that there be no rain, and that the land yield not her fruit; and lest ye perish quickly from off the good land which the LORD giveth you." In Israel the early rain would germinate the seed and start the growth of the plant, and then the latter rain would finish its growth and prepare it for the harvest. In order to receive the early and latter rain they were told that they must hearken to the Lord's commandments and love Him and serve Him. The same is true in the spiritual application as well. Now, as we approach the end of this world, we must be developing a strong love relationship with Jesus, completely following His Ten Commandments, and serving Him. This will allow the Early Rain to do its work, so that we can receive the Latter Rain.

Ellen White warns us of this in *Early Writings*, p. 71. *"I saw that many were neglecting the preparation so needful and were looking to the time of "refreshing" and the "latter rain" to fit them to stand in the day of the Lord and to live in His sight. Oh, how many I saw in the time of trouble without a shelter! They had neglected the needful preparation; therefore they could not receive the refreshing that all must have to fit them to live in the sight of a holy God."* The theme that stands out as we study these Final Events is that we must draw closer and closer to Jesus. He loves us so much and wants us to draw very close to Him so that He can prepare us for His Second Coming, through the work of the Holy Spirit, known as the Early Rain. He wants us to spend time with Him, to put ourselves in the atmosphere in which the Holy Spirit can work, and do so on a daily basis. He wants us to allow Him to speak to us through the study of His Word and to talk back to Him in prayer. He wants us to depend on Him moment by moment. He wants us to cooperate with Him and allow Him constantly to be our Lord. And then, He wants to give us the Latter Rain, which will finish the work in us, assist us with the Loud Cry, and prepare us to go through the time of the

Seven Last Plagues, the Great Time of Trouble. Friend, won't you make a concerted effort to spend time with Jesus every day, to allow Him to prepare you for the Latter Rain and His Second Coming?

In other churches there are many well-meaning preachers who will tell you that there is absolutely nothing that you need to do for salvation, absolutely nothing; God does it all for us. This statement is a half-truth and is very misleading and dangerous. For example, when you go to the dentist who does the work? The dentist does, of course. However, we must make the appointment with him. When we arrive, we must sit in the dentist's chair and cooperate with him. We must spend the time with him, allowing him to counsel us concerning our dental problems, and then allow him to do the work needed to correct the problems. The same thing must occur in our relationship with Jesus Christ. We must make the appointment with Him to spend quality time with Him on a daily basis, allowing Him to counsel us concerning our sins and problems. We then must cooperate with Him, and allow Him to do the work that heaven wants to do in us to correct those sins and problems and prepare us for the Second Coming of Christ.

The Spirit of Prophecy states in *Testimonies to Ministers and Gospel Workers*, p. 508, *"We may have had a measure of the Spirit of God, but by prayer and faith we are continually to seek more of the Spirit. It will never do to cease our efforts. If we do not progress, if we do not place ourselves in an attitude to receive both the former and the latter rain, we shall lose our souls, and the responsibility will lie at our own door."* She warns us here that we must place ourselves in an attitude to receive the Early and the Latter Rain. We must make a conscious effort to place ourselves in the atmosphere to receive the Early Rain through our relationship with Jesus Christ. We must spend less time with interests that detract from our time with God and more time with Jesus, studying His Word, and talking to Him in prayer. The Spirit is enabled, then, to work on our minds and hearts in Early Rain power to prepare us for the reception of the Latter Rain as we approach the end of this world.

What measure of the Latter Rain power will each of us receive? Well, every person will receive a measure of the Latter Rain power proportioned according to certain conditions. Those conditions were mentioned in the *Review and Herald*, May 5, 1896. *"The measure of the*

Holy Spirit we receive, will be proportioned to the measure of our desire and the faith exercised for it, and the use we shall make of the light and knowledge that shall be given to us. We shall be entrusted with the Holy Spirit according to our capacity to receive and our ability to impart it to others." The first two conditions that determine the measure of the Holy Spirit we receive are our desire to receive both the Early and Latter Rain and the faith exercised for it. Friend, do you want to receive the Early and Latter Rain? Are you exercising your faith now through your relationship with God to receive the Early Rain power? Are you allowing Jesus to change you to be more like He is through the work of the Holy Spirit, thereby preparing you for these Final Events? Do you have the faith to believe that God will give the Latter Rain power to you?

In addition, our measure of the Holy Spirit we receive under the Latter Rain power will depend first on the use we will make of the light given to us, then on our capacity to receive and understand the light and knowledge given to us, and, finally, on our ability to impart that light to others. The first question we must ask ourselves is, what are we doing with the light given to us now under the Early Rain power? Are we willing to share that light with others? Do we now understand the light given to us and have the ability to impart that light to others? Are we now actively engaged in sharing that light by giving Bible studies to others? Are we increasing our ability, through the Holy Spirit, to share that light with others?

From these Spirit of Prophecy statements there is one conclusion we may immediately draw. The training ground to prepare for the Latter Rain is now! We must now be learning how to understand God's truths and impart His truths to other people. We must now be willing to give Bible studies to others and learn the answers to questions that individuals might ask. We must now be involved in the Lord's work, experiencing the Lord working through us to impart His truths to other people, thereby gaining an understanding of how to present most effectively those biblical truths we hold so dear to our hearts. This preparation will enhance our ability to impart God's truths to others. Through this preparation for the Latter Rain power we will receive a greater measure of the Holy Spirit, as that Latter Rain power is given to God's people as we approach the end of the world. The Holy Spirit will then enhance our presentations to such a degree that the results will be beyond belief.

Another condition for the reception of the Latter Rain was revealed in the *Review and Herald*, July 20, 1886. *"May the Lord help his people to cleanse the soul temple from every defilement, and to maintain such a close connection with him that they may be partakers of the latter rain when it shall be poured out."* Our soul temple must be cleansed from every defilement, and this is accomplished by the Holy Spirit through our connection and relationship with God under the Early Rain power. All we have to do is spend the time with heaven and allow heaven to do the work.

This principle is expanded in the *Review and Herald*, March 22, 1892. "It is Not for You to Know the Times and the Seasons". *"Today you are to give yourselves to God that he may make of you vessels unto honor, and meet for his service. Today you are to give yourself to God, that you may be emptied of self, emptied of envy, jealousy, evil-surmising, strife, everything that shall be dishonoring to God. Today you are to have your vessel purified that it may be ready for the heavenly dew, ready for the showers of the latter rain; for the latter rain will come, and the blessing of God will fill every soul that is purified from every defilement. It is our work today to yield our souls to Christ, that we may be fitted for the time of refreshing from the presence of the Lord—fitted for the baptism of the Holy Spirit."*

We have seen in several statements that we must be purified from every defilement to receive the Latter Rain. In a moment you will see a statement that says we need to perfect holiness in the fear of God to receive the Latter Rain. All of this is accomplished through the Early Rain power. The question that comes to my mind and probably to yours is where does the Latter Rain come into this process? We are given a picture of the entire process in *Testimonies to Ministers and Gospel Workers*, p. 507. *"Many have in a great measure failed to receive the former rain. They have not obtained all the benefits that God has thus provided for them. They expect that the lack will be supplied by the latter rain. When the richest abundance of grace shall be bestowed, they intend to open their hearts to receive it. They are making a terrible mistake. The work that God has begun in the human heart in giving His light and knowledge must be continually going forward. Every individ-*

ual must realize his own necessity. The heart must be emptied of every defilement and cleansed for the indwelling of the Spirit. It was by the confession and forsaking of sin, by earnest prayer and consecration of themselves to God, that the early disciples prepared for the outpouring of the Holy Spirit on the Day of Pentecost. The same work, only in greater degree, must be done now. Then the human agent had only to ask for the blessing, and wait for the Lord to perfect the work concerning him. It is God who began the work, and He will finish His work, making man complete in Jesus Christ. But there must be no neglect of the grace represented by the former rain." As the disciples did, we must now confess and forsake all sin, earnestly pray and consecrate ourselves to God, to cleanse and purify ourselves of every defilement, through the power of the Holy Spirit, under the Early Rain. Then we must ask for the Latter Rain power and wait for the Lord to perfect the work concerning us. This will enable us to proclaim the Third Angel's Message with great power during the Little Time of Trouble.

There is another aspect of this cleansing and purification that also must occur to prepare us for the reception of the Latter Rain. While this aspect is implied in previous passages, it is better understood as described in *Counsels on Diet and Foods*, p. 33. *"I was shown that if God's people make no efforts on their part, but wait for the refreshing to come upon them and remove their wrongs and correct their errors; if they depend upon that to cleanse them from filthiness of the flesh and spirit, and fit them to engage in the loud cry of the third angel, they will be found wanting. The refreshing or power of God comes only on those who have prepared themselves for it by doing the work which God bids them, namely, cleansing themselves from all filthiness of the flesh and spirit, perfecting holiness in the fear of God."* From this statement it is clear that those who receive the Latter Rain and give the Loud Cry, a group we call the 144,000, must first be cleansed from the filthiness of the flesh and spirit. We have discovered previously that we are cleansed from the filthiness of the spirit via our relationship with God as we surrender to Jesus and allow the Holy Spirit to work in our hearts as He leads us toward holiness. However, for God to do this we also must be cleansed and purified of filthiness of the flesh. How do we cleanse and purify ourselves of filthiness of the flesh? The answer to this question is found in the role of health reform as we approach the end of this world.

The Role of Health Reform

In *Testimonies for the Church*, Vol. 9, p.112 is the following statement. *"The work of health reform is the Lord's means for lessening suffering in our world and for purifying His church."* By the work of health reform God purifies the physical aspect of human beings. This physical purification facilitates spiritual purification, as God makes His people a holy people.

In *Counsels on Diet and Foods*, p. 36, is the following statement. *"I am instructed to bear a message to all our people on the subject of health reform; for many have backslidden from their former loyalty to health reform principles.*

God's purpose for His children is that they shall grow up to the full stature of men and women in Christ. In order to do this, they must use aright every power of mind, soul, and body. They cannot afford to waste any mental or physical strength.

The question of how to preserve the health is one of primary importance. When we study this question in the fear of God, we shall learn that it is best, for both our physical and our spiritual advancement, to observe simplicity in diet. Let us patiently study this question. We need knowledge and judgment in order to move wisely in this matter. Nature's laws are not to be resisted, but obeyed.

Those who have received instruction regarding the evils of the use of flesh foods, tea, and coffee, and rich and unhealthful food preparations, and who are determined to make a covenant with God by sacrifice, will not continue to indulge their appetite for food that they know to be unhealthful. God demands that the appetites be cleansed, and that self-denial be practiced in regard to those things which are not good. This is a work that will have to be done before His people can stand before Him a perfected people."

Brother or sister in Christ, we need to take seriously the role of health reform as we approach the end of this world, amen? Obviously, in the cleansing of the flesh, a healthy diet plays a huge role. In the above quotation some of the culprits of a healthy diet are mentioned. There is no question in Seventh-day Adventist circles concerning the evils of the use of tea, coffee, and rich and unhealthful food preparations in today's diet. However, regarding the use of meat in today's diet there is great controversy.

Now friend, I would be neglectful in writing a book about the Final Events without letting you know the warnings in the Spirit of Prophecy concerning the consumption of meat as we approach the end of this planet. What you do with this information is between you and the Lord. We are, however, admonished extensively in the Spirit of Prophecy to stop the eating of meat as we approach the end of this world.

Some of the reasons are given in *Testimonies for the Church*, Vol. 2, p. 64. *"The liability to take disease is increased tenfold by meat eating. The intellectual, the moral, and the physical powers are depreciated by the habitual use of flesh meats. Meat eating deranges the system, beclouds the intellect, and blunts the moral sensibilities."*

There has never been a time in which the liability to take disease by meat eating has been greater than right now. Elson M. Haas, M.D., addresses this in his book *Staying Healthy with Nutrition*, p. 347. He states that the free-ranging animals of the past that lived naturally on vegetation had a much lower fat content than present-day animals that are "force-fed on lots of grains with less activity." "Cancer rates are increased with the higher amounts of dietary fats, which many studies relate particularly to colon, rectal, and breast cancer, though the risk of other types of cancer is probably increased as well." Cured meats such as lunch meat and franks, with their higher fat content, also contain cancer-causing chemicals such as nitrates.

Chicken and cattle are given stimulants, antibiotics, and growth hormones.

"Medical concerns over beef include increased cholesterol levels, high blood pressure, and atherosclerosis. This may lead to coronary artery disease and heart attacks or strokes." [5]

A warning about the danger of continuing the practice of meat-eating as we approach the end of this world is given in *Maranatha*, p. 62, as follows. *"Greater reforms should be seen among the people who claim to be looking for the soon appearing of Christ. Health reform is to do among our people a work which it has not yet done. There are those who ought to be awake to the danger of meat-eating, who are still eating the flesh of animals, thus endangering the physical, mental, and spiritual health. Many who are now only half converted on the question of meat-eating will go from God's people, to walk no more with them.*

'The controlling power of appetite will prove the ruin of thousands, when, if they had conquered on this point, they would have had moral power to gain the victory over every other temptation of Satan. But those who are slaves to appetite will fail in perfecting Christian character. The continual transgression of man for six thousand years has brought sickness, pain, and death as its fruits. And as we near the close of time, Satan's temptation to indulge appetite will be more powerful and more difficult to overcome.

Again and again I have been shown that God is trying to lead us back, step by step, to His original design—that man should subsist upon the natural products of the earth. Among those who are waiting for the coming of the Lord, meat-eating will eventually be done away; flesh will cease to form a part of their diet. We should ever keep this end in view, and endeavor to work steadily toward it."

Further warning is given in *Testimony Studies on Diet and Foods*, p. 65. *"Those who claim to believe the truth are to guard carefully the powers of body and mind, so that God and His cause will not be in any way dishonored by their words or actions. The habits and practices are to be brought into subjection to the will of God. We are to give careful attention to our diet. It has been clearly presented to me that God's people are to take a firm stand against meat-eating. Would God for thirty years give His people the message that if they desire to have pure blood and clear minds, they must give up the use of flesh-meat if He did not want them to heed this message? By the use of flesh-meats the animal nature is strengthened and the spiritual nature weakened. Such men as you, who are engaged in the most solemn and important work ever entrusted to human beings, need to give special heed what they eat."*

These statements give us quite a warning concerning the intake of flesh foods as we approach the end of this world. From these accounts it is obvious that if we wait to depend on the Latter Rain to cleanse us from the filthiness of the flesh and spirit and to prepare us to give the Loud Cry, it will be too late. We must now be working with God to discard unhealthful foods and practices and consume nourishing, healthful foods and herbs that will yield a healthy body and clear mind. The Holy Spirit will then be able to work in a mighty way during the time of the Early Rain, through our relationship with God, as we are cleansed from filthiness of the flesh and spirit and prepared to receive the Latter Rain as it is poured out, which will enable the Lord to use us as great instruments in His work as we approach the end of the world.

The Counsel of the True Witness

What is the Counsel of the True Witness, and how does it fit into the Latter Rain picture? The Counsel of the True Witness is mentioned in *Testimonies*, Vol.1, p.187, as follows: *"Those who come up to every point, and stand every test, and overcome be the price what it may, have heeded the counsel of the True Witness, and they will receive the latter rain, and thus be fitted for translation."* The Counsel of the True Witness is counsel that is heeded by those who receive the Latter Rain.

What is this counsel? Revelation 3:14-22 (NKJV) gives us the counsel. *"And to the angel of the church of the Laodiceans write, 'These things says the Amen, the Faithful and True Witness, the Beginning of the creation of God: "I know your works, that you are neither cold nor hot. I could wish you were cold or hot. "So then, because you are lukewarm, and neither cold nor hot, I will spew you out of My mouth. "Because you say, 'I am rich, have become wealthy, and have need of nothing'—and do not know that you are wretched, miserable, poor, blind, and naked–"I counsel you to buy from Me gold refined in the fire, that you may be rich; and white garments, that you may be clothed, that the shame of your nakedness may not be revealed; and anoint your eyes with eye salve, that you may see."* This is the Counsel of the True Witness, who, of course, is Jesus Christ Himself. The counsel is to stop being a lukewarm Christian; buy from Me gold refined (*tried*, KJV) in the fire that you may be rich and white garments (*raiment*, KJV) that you may be clothed, and eye salve that you may see.

What is the gold refined in the fire and the white raiment we are counseled to buy, and the eye salve we are to anoint our eyes with, all of which will enable us to "stand every test, and overcome be the price what it may," and therefore receive the Latter Rain.? The Spirit of

Prophecy gives us the answer in *Testimonies for the Church*, Vol. 5, p. 233. *"Again and again has the voice from heaven addressed you. Will you obey this voice? Will you heed the counsel of the True Witness to seek the gold tried in the fire, the white raiment, and the eyesalve? The gold is faith and love, the white raiment is the righteousness of Christ, the eyesalve is that spiritual discernment which will enable you to see the wiles of Satan and shun them, to detect sin and abhor it, to see truth and obey it."* How do we seek the gold, the white raiment, and the eye salve? How are these items given to us? This is accomplished through our relationship with Jesus, as we spend the time with Him, do our part and cooperate with Him, and allow Him to change us to be more like He is. He wants to try us in the fire to purify our character and give us a strong measure of faith and love; to put the white raiment, His righteousness, on us; to anoint our eyes through the work of the Holy Spirit that we may see our sins and repent from them, and see the truth and obey it. This He accomplishes through our relationship with Him. This is the Counsel of the True Witness: to spend the time with Jesus and allow Him to help us overcome sin, and to allow Him to prepare us for these Final Events and for the end of the world.

Jesus continues in verse 19, *"As many as I love, I rebuke and chasten. Therefore be zealous and repent. "Behold, I stand at the door and knock. If anyone hears My voice and opens the door, I will come in to him and dine with him, and he with Me. "To him who overcomes I will grant to sit with Me on My throne, as I also overcame and sat down with My Father on His throne." He who has an ear, let him hear what the Spirit says to the churches."'"* Whoever heeds the Counsel of the True Witness and develops a strong relationship with Jesus, thereby overcoming sin, will be granted the privilege of sitting with Jesus on His throne.

Jesus gives this warning concerning overcoming sin to all of the seven churches and gives a different promise of reward to each church for those that overcome. Why do you think there is so much emphasis on overcoming sin? It is because those who overcome do so as a result of their relationship with Jesus! We cannot overcome sin on our own. We need Jesus in our lives to overcome, just as Jesus needed the Father in His life to keep from sinning when He lived as a human being here on earth. Overcoming sin demonstrates to the angels in heaven and all beings from the unfallen worlds that the relationship with Jesus is present, that Jesus is purifying that individual's character, that Jesus is clothing that individual with His righteousness, and that those individuals who possess that relationship are worthy of salvation, are worthy of the Latter Rain, and worthy of a residence in heaven.

Ellen White expounded on this in *Early Writings*, p. 71. *"I saw that none could share the 'refreshing' unless they obtain the victory over every besetment, over pride, selfishness, love of the world, and over every wrong word and action. We should, therefore, be drawing nearer and nearer to the Lord and be earnestly seeking that preparation necessary to enable us to stand in the battle in the day of the Lord."* We need to heed the Counsel of the True Witness, Jesus Himself, and enter into that close relationship with Him, allowing Him to help us overcome sin and prepare us for the Final Events and for His second coming.

The Spirit of Prophecy explains the gold tried in the fire in *Gospel Workers*, pp. 418,419. *"Every one needs a practical experience in trusting God for himself. Let no man become your confessor; open the heart to God; tell Him every secret of the soul. Bring to Him your difficulties, small and great, and He will show you a way out of them all. He alone can know how to give the very help you need.*

And when, after a trying season, help comes to you, when the Spirit of God is manifestly at work for you, what a precious experience you gain! You are obtaining faith and love, the gold that the True Witness counsels you to buy of Him. You are learning to go to God in all your troubles; and as you learn these precious lessons of faith, you will teach the same to others. Thus you may be continually leading the people to a higher plane of experience."

The Spirit of Prophecy explains the putting on of the white raiment in *Christ's Object Lessons*, p. 312. *"When we submit ourselves to Christ, the heart is united with His heart, the will is merged in His will, the mind becomes one with His mind, the thoughts are brought into captivity to Him; we live His life. This is what it means to be clothed with the garment of His righteousness. Then as the Lord looks upon us He sees, not the fig-leaf garment, not the nakedness and deformity of sin, but His own robe of righteousness, which is perfect obedience to the law of Jehovah."* Again, we must draw nearer and nearer to the Lord, develop a strong relationship with Him, gain a greater experience with Him, and thereby develop faith and love, the gold tried in the fire. In the process, as we submit to Him, Jesus will put on us the white raiment, His righteousness, and the Spirit will give us the eye salve, that we may have spiritual discernment! Amen!

The Putting Away of Dissension

A natural outcome of drawing nearer and nearer to the Lord is the putting away of all dissension. In *Testimonies*, Vol. 8, p. 21, is the following: *"Let Christians put away all dissension and give themselves to God for the saving of the lost. Let them ask in faith for the promised blessing, and it will come. The outpouring of the Spirit in the days of the apostles was "the former rain," and glorious was the result. But the latter rain will be more abundant."* To receive the Latter Rain we must put away all dissension, which is a natural result of a close relationship with Jesus, and then ask in faith for that promised blessing.

We also must give ourselves to God for the saving of the lost. As we work for the salvation of other souls we naturally come close to Jesus as we pray for those individuals, do the necessary preparation to share with them, help them through their problems, and learn to depend on heaven and the work of the Holy Spirit for their salvation, since we ourselves cannot convert their minds or their hearts. Working for the salvation of the lost naturally brings us closer to Jesus, probably more than any other aspect of the Christian walk with God, since we must depend totally on Jesus for their salvation.

Ellen White expands our understanding of this prerequisite for the Latter Rain in *Christian Service*, p. 253. *"The great outpouring of the Spirit of God, which lightens the whole earth with His glory, will not come until we have an enlightened people, that know by experience what it means to be laborers together with God. When we have entire, wholehearted consecration to the service of Christ, God will recognize the fact by an outpouring of His Spirit without measure; but this will not be while the largest portion of the church are not laborers together with God."* Our Lord wants us to be in His service, working for the salvation of other individuals, as we approach the end of this world. Our

Lord is able to work in a more dramatic way upon our minds and hearts as we engage ourselves in service for Him.

For example, if you were to read the gospel every day, which really is required if you want to have a close walk with Jesus, it is well known and proven that you will retain up to ten percent of what you have read. However, it is also well known and proven that if you were to teach that same gospel to someone else, you will retain up to ninety percent of what you have read and taught. Due to the fact you are retaining much more of the gospel, the Holy Spirit is then able to lead you into following the additional biblical principles you are accepting and retaining, thereby changing you to be more like Jesus at a much faster rate. We grow as Christians exponentially when we are involved in the teaching of the gospel of Jesus Christ. No wonder Jesus commanded us, *"Go ye therefore, and teach all nations, baptizing them in the name of the Father, and of the Son, and of the Holy Ghost: Teaching them to observe all things whatsoever I have commanded you"* (Matt. 28:19, 20).

We are told in the Spirit of Prophecy that the majority of us must be laborers together with God for the salvation of souls before the Holy Spirit is poured out in the Latter Rain. The Spirit of Prophecy is very strong on this point. In *Christian Service*, p. 253, is the statement, *"Those who make no decided effort, but simply wait for the Holy Spirit to compel them to action, will perish in darkness. You are not to sit still and do nothing in the work of God."*

Summary of Requirements for the Latter Rain

We have found that there are several requirements for the reception of the Latter Rain revealed in the Bible and the Spirit of Prophecy. Many times in our churches these requirements are ignored and we are told to just pray for the Latter Rain. However, to receive the Latter Rain we must be developing a strong daily relationship with Jesus, submitting to Him completely, cooperating with Him, allowing Him through the Holy Spirit to give us victory over the sins that beset us, cleanse the soul temple spiritually, and to mold our character for heaven, thereby heeding the Counsel of the True Witness. As a result, dissension between us will be put away.

In addition, we must cleanse the soul temple physically, as we maintain a healthy body by following health principles outlined in the Word of God and health reform principles outlined in the Spirit of Prophecy.

We also must give ourselves to God for the saving of the lost. We must now be learning how to understand God's truths and how to impart His truths to other people. This would be done by giving Bible studies to individuals now! Our training ground is now! This experience must be gained now!

Before the disciples received the Early Rain in the upper room, they experienced how to impart God's truths to other people, as Jesus taught them and then sent them out, as recorded in Matthew 10 and Luke 10. We must also gain the experience of sharing God's truths with other individuals, which will prepare us for the reception of the Latter Rain in which the Holy Spirit, in a mighty way, will enhance our presentations to others. The Holy Spirit is able to work in a much more dramatic way if we are experienced in the sharing of the gospel than if we are not experienced at all. During the Latter Rain, the Holy Spirit does not teach us how to defend our faith. The Holy Spirit enhances the presentations we make in defense of our faith.

For example, if you were to give Bible studies to an Evangelical Christian, when you taught the biblical concept of the Second Coming of Jesus, you would immediately be confronted with an objection because Evangelicals believe in the Secret Rapture and the Seven Year Tribulation. If, due to the fact you have never given a Bible study and heard that objection, and therefore are not sure where to turn in the Scriptures to defend your faith, you would not know what to say. However, now that you have heard that objection, you go home and research the biblical answer, and then go back and share the answer with that individual, you have gained a priceless experience through which the Holy Spirit can use you in a mighty way, should that objection be brought up when the Latter Rain is poured out and we are approaching the end of the world. We must be gaining these experiences of being laborers together with God for the salvation of souls. Through these experiences God will teach us how to impart His truths to others, and this will prepare us for a much greater measure of the Holy Spirit to be poured out upon us in the Latter Rain as we approach the end of this world. The Holy Spirit will then give us the words through recall of those experiences, enhance our presentation, and make that presentation much more effective than it had ever been previously. Amen.

The Loud Cry

Those who receive the Latter Rain will be giving the Loud Cry as we approach the end of this world. What is this cry about? Revelation 14:9,10 tells us, *"And the third angel followed them, saying with a loud voice* [the Loud Cry], *If any man worship the beast and his image, and receive his mark in his forehead, or in his hand, The same shall drink of the wine of the wrath of God, which is poured out without mixture into the cup of his indignation; and he shall be tormented with fire and brimstone in the presence of the holy angels, and in the presence of the Lamb."* The Loud Cry gives the warning to not worship the beast, the Papal Roman kingdom, or his image, Apostate Protestantism, and receive the Mark of the Beast, a mark given to those who accept the beast's false teaching and worship on the Venerable Day of the Sun, or you will receive the wrath of God. What is the wrath of God? The Bible tells us it is the Seven Last Plagues (Rev. 15:1).

Revelation 18:1-5 further expands our understanding of this Loud Cry. *"And after these things I saw another angel come down from heaven, having great power; and the earth was lightened with his glory. And he cried mightily with a strong voice, saying, Babylon the great is fallen, is fallen, and is become the habitation of devils, and the hold of every foul spirit, and a cage of every unclean and hateful bird. For all nations have drunk of the wine of the wrath of her fornication, and the kings of the earth have committed fornication with her, and the merchants of the earth are waxed rich through the abundance of her delicacies. And I heard another voice from heaven, saying, Come out of her, my people, that ye be not partakers of her sins, and that ye receive not of her plagues."* The Loud Cry message is that Babylon is fallen. Don't worship Papal Rome or Apostate Protestantism or receive its mark. It has committed fornication against God by spreading its false doctrines and thereby deceiving the nations. Come out of Babylon! Observe all of God's Ten Commandments, including God's Sabbath. Don't receive the Seven Last Plagues!

The Latter Rain is given to assist in the Loud Cry to the world. *Early Writings*, p. 271, gives us the results. *"I heard those clothed with the armor speak forth the truth with great power. It had effect. Many had been bound; some wives by their husbands, and some children by their parents. The honest who had been prevented from hearing the truth now eagerly laid hold upon it. All fear of their relatives was gone, and the truth alone was exalted to them. They had been hungering and thirsting for truth; it was dearer and more precious than life. I asked what had made this great change. An angel answered, It is the latter rain, the refreshing from the presence of the Lord, the loud cry of the third angel."*

Many individuals who have heard the truth previously, through Bible studies, seminars, and crusades, but did not take their stand for the truth because of the influence of family and friends, or who have been prevented from hearing all of the truth by their family and friends, or other circumstances, now, during the Loud Cry, take hold of the truth presented through the power and influence of the Holy Spirit, and stand up for Jesus Christ.

This time period is further described in *The Great Controversy* (1911), p. 612, *"The message will be carried not so much by argument as by the deep conviction of the Spirit of God. The arguments have been presented. The seed has been sown, and now it will spring up and bear fruit. The publications distributed by missionary workers have exerted their influence, yet many whose minds were impressed have been prevented from fully comprehending the truth or from yielding obedience. Now the rays of light penetrate everywhere, the truth is seen in its clearness, and the honest children of God sever the bands which have held them. Family connections, church relations, are powerless to stay them now. Truth is more precious than all besides. Notwithstanding the agencies combined against the truth, a large number take their stand upon the Lord's side."*

In *Early Writings*, p. 33, we find the timing of the Loud Cry. *"And at the commencement of the time of trouble, we were filled with the Holy Ghost as we went forth and proclaimed the Sabbath more fully."* This statement puts the Loud Cry beginning at the commencement of the time of trouble, which must be the Little Time of Trouble, while probation is still open.

In *Evangelism*, p. 694, is the following statement. *"During the loud cry, the church, aided by the providential interpositions of her exalted Lord, will diffuse the knowledge of salvation so abundantly that light will be communicated to every city and town. The earth will be filled with the knowledge of salvation. So abundantly will the renewing Spirit of God have crowned with success the intensely active agencies, that the light of present truth will be seen flashing everywhere."* Amen! This will be quite a remarkable event!

How many will be converted at this time? In *The Ellen G. White 1888 Materials*, p. 755, is the following quotation. *"There will be thousands converted to the truth in a day who at the eleventh hour see and acknowledge the truth and the movements of the Spirit of God."*

The Great Controversy, p. 606, sums up the Latter Rain and the Loud Cry this way. *"Thus the message of the third angel will be proclaimed. As the time comes for it to be given with greatest power, the Lord will work through humble instruments, leading the minds of those who consecrate themselves to His service. The laborers will be qualified rather by the unction of His Spirit than by the training of literary institutions. Men of faith and prayer will be constrained to go forth with holy zeal, declaring the words which God gives them. The sins of Babylon will be laid open. The fearful results of enforcing the observances of the church by civil authority, the inroads of spiritualism, the stealthy but rapid progress of the papal power—all will be unmasked. By these solemn warnings the people will be stirred. Thousands upon thousands will listen who have never heard words like these. In amazement they hear the testimony that Babylon is the church, fallen because of her errors and sins, because of her rejection of the truth sent to her from heaven."*

Summary of Requirements for the Loud Cry

I want to be a part of the Loud Cry! I want to receive the Latter Rain, don't you? However the Spirit of Prophecy is clear concerning the requirements to be part of these Final Events. We must develop a close relationship with Jesus and allow His Spirit to help us overcome sin and become holy people. In *Bible Training School*, Dec.1, 1903 is the following statement. *"The world can only be warned by seeing those who believe the truth sanctified through the truth, acting upon high and holy principles, showing in a high, elevated sense, the line of demarcation between those who keep the commandments of God, and those who trample them under their feet. The sanctification of the Spirit signalizes the difference between those who have the seal of God, and those who keep a spurious rest-day."* We need to be sanctified by heaven through a close relationship with Jesus Christ to be a part of the Loud Cry.

We also need to be involved in the proclamation of the gospel, being laborers together with God for the salvation of souls. In *Evangelism*, p. 692, is the following statement. *"The end is near, stealing upon us stealthily, imperceptibly, like the noiseless approach of a thief in the night. May the Lord grant that we shall no longer sleep as do others, but that we shall watch and be sober. The truth is soon to triumph gloriously, and all who now choose to be laborers together with God, will triumph with it. The time is short; the night soon cometh when no man can work."*

The False Latter Rain

The Spirit of Prophecy also informs us of a False Latter Rain that will come prior to the Latter Rain. In *Early Writings*, p. 261, the Spirit of Prophecy states, *"God has honest children among the nominal Adventists and the fallen churches, and before the plagues shall be poured out, ministers and people will be called out from these churches and will gladly receive the truth. Satan knows this; and before the loud cry of the third angel is given, he raises an excitement in these religious bodies, that those who have rejected the truth may think that God is with them. He hopes to deceive the honest and lead them to think that God is still working for the churches."*

In *The Great Controversy*, p. 464, is the following: *"Before the final visitation of God's judgments upon the earth there will be among the people of the Lord such a revival of primitive godliness as has not been witnessed since apostolic times. The Spirit and power of God will be poured out upon His children. At that time many will separate themselves from those churches in which the love of this world has supplanted love for God and His word. Many, both of ministers and people, will gladly accept those great truths which God has caused to be proclaimed at this time to prepare a people for the Lord's second coming. The enemy of souls desires to hinder this work; and before the time for such a movement shall come, he will endeavor to prevent it by introducing a counterfeit. In those churches which he can bring under his deceptive power he will make it appear that God's special blessing is poured out; there will be manifest what is thought to be great religious interest. Multitudes will exult that God is working marvelously for them, when the work is that of another spirit. Under a religious guise, Satan will seek to extend his influence over the Christian world."*

And in *Early Writings*, p. 261, we find, *"Some look with horror upon one deception, while they readily receive another. Satan deceives some with Spiritualism. He also comes as an angel of light and spreads his influence over the land by means of false reformations. The churches are elated, and consider that God is working marvelously for them, when it is the work of another spirit."* From these statements we know there will be a False Latter Rain just prior to the genuine Latter Rain as we approach the end of this world. As this False Latter Rain falls, may each one of us be prepared and ready to receive the true Latter Rain from the Holy Spirit.

Chapter 4

The Little Time of Trouble: the Shaking, the Coming of Satan and the Evil Angels, the Second Sunday Law

As we consider the Little Time of Trouble, let's review and further expand on what we have learned thus far. We are told that as the National Sunday Law is agitated we must do everything we can to keep it from becoming law, to allow us to proclaim the gospel for as long as possible without persecution. This aspect is commented on in *Testimonies*, Vol. 5, p. 714. *"We are not doing the will of God if we sit in quietude, doing nothing to preserve liberty of conscience. Fervent, effectual prayer should be ascending to heaven that this calamity may be deferred until we can accomplish the work which has so long been neglected. Let there be most earnest prayer and then let us work in harmony with our prayers."*

As we seek to delay the enactment of the National Sunday Law, the Spirit of Prophecy informs us of two reasons that are utilized to encourage the establishment of this Sunday law. (As mentioned earlier, neither of these reasons pertain to a collapse of the United States economy.) The first of these reasons is explained in *Manuscript Release 10*, p. 239. *"Satan puts his interpretation upon events, and they think, as he would have them, that the calamities which fill the land are a result of Sunday-breaking. Thinking to appease the wrath of God these influential men make laws enforcing Sunday observance."*

The second reason given for the enactment of the National Sunday Law is specified in *The Great Controversy*, p. 587. *"This very class put forth the claim that the fast-spreading corruption is largely attributable to the desecration of the so-called "Christian sabbath" and that the enforcement of Sunday observance would greatly improve the morals of society. This claim is especially urged in America, where the doctrine of the true Sabbath has been most widely preached."* They blame the increase of calamities and the fast-spreading corruption throughout America on Sunday-breaking, and use these reasons as the basis for the enactment of a National Sunday Law.

We learned earlier that once the National Sunday Law is enacted, it tosses us into the Little Time of Trouble, a time period in which this national apostasy in the United States will quickly be followed by national ruin. This enactment of the National Sunday Law is the Abomination That Causes Desolation. God's dealing with human beings changes as great natural disasters, greater than we have ever seen before, as well as economic ruin, then occur.

This time period is summarized in *Fundamentals of Christian Education*, pp. 356,357. *"Do you believe that the Lord is coming, and that the last great crisis is about to break upon the world? There will soon be a sudden change in God's dealings. The world in its perversity is being visited by casualties,—by floods, storms, fires, earthquakes, famines, wars, and bloodshed. The Lord is slow to anger, and great in power . . . But His forbearance will not always continue. Who is prepared for the sudden change that will take place in God's dealing with sinful men?"* We have recently seen many casualties on this planet— great hurricanes and their disastrous effects, a tsunami in which hundreds of thousands were killed, earthquakes in different places, (At this writing, the Haiti earthquake has killed more than 200,000), great fires throughout the world, famines in different parts of the world causing starvation and the death of thousands, wars and bloodshed in different areas of the world, etc. However, there is a time period on the horizon worse than this, as we enter the Little Time of Trouble and God changes his way of dealing with sinful men. Great natural disasters, greater than we have ever experienced before will occur. There will be economic disaster in these United States as well. All of this is triggered by the National Sunday Law, the Abomination That Causes Desolation.

We are also warned that when this National Sunday Law is enacted here in the United States, and subsequently enacted in many other countries of the world, we are to get out of the cities and flee to the more rural areas, since the natural disasters will occur largely in the wicked cities. *Evangelism*, p. 27, reveals the following: *"I am bidden to declare the message that cities full of transgression, and sinful in the extreme, will be destroyed by earthquakes, by fire, by flood. All the world will be warned that there is a God who will display His authority as God. His unseen agencies will cause destruction, devastation, and death. All the accumulated riches will be as nothingness. . . .*

Calamities will come—calamities most awful, most unexpected; and these destructions will follow one after another . . . Strictly will the cities of the nations be dealt with, and yet they will not be visited in the extreme of God's indignation, because some souls will yet break away from the delusions of the enemy, and will repent and be converted, while the mass will be treasuring up wrath against the day of wrath." This will not be the worst of the scourges God is going to bring upon humankind. The worst scourges will come during the Great Time of Trouble, under the Seven Last Plagues, when the wrath of God is poured out upon mankind unmixed with mercy.

The Great Controversy, p. 629, says, *"All the judgments upon men, prior to the close of probation, have been mingled with mercy. . . . but in the final judgment, wrath is poured out unmixed with mercy."* Even though they are mingled with mercy these will be devastating disasters, great natural disasters the likes of which we have never seen before on this planet.

Also, during this time period, in addition to moving out of the cities, we are encouraged to go where the opportunity to preach and teach the gospel is favorable, as stated in *Ellen G. White Manuscript 26* as follows: *"As enmity is aroused in various places against those who observe the Sabbath of the Lord, it may become necessary for God's people to move from those places to places where they will not be so bitterly opposed.*

God does not require His children to remain where, by the course of wicked men, their influence is made of no effect and their lives endangered. When liberty and life are imperiled it is not merely our priv-

ilege, it is our positive duty to go to places where the people are willing to hear the Word of life and where the opportunities for preaching the Word will be more favorable."

Cross-Examined for our Faith

As these natural disasters fall and the Loud Cry is given, many of us will be cross-examined for our faith. The question, then, will be, are we prepared to be cross-examined for our faith? If not, we are told in *Testimonies*, Vol. 5, p. 707, *"I have been shown that many who profess to have a knowledge of present truth know not what they believe. They do not understand the evidences of their faith. They have no just appreciation of the work for the present time. When the time of trial shall come, there are men now preaching to others who will find, upon examining the positions they hold, that there are many things for which they can give no satisfactory reason. Until thus tested they knew not their great ignorance. And there are many in the church who take it for granted that they understand what they believe; but, until controversy arises, they do not know their own weakness. When separated from those of like faith and compelled to stand singly and alone to explain their belief, they will be surprised to see how confused are their ideas of what they had accepted as truth."* We are warned here that we must know what we believe and why we believe it in order to defend our faith as we approach the end of this world. The easiest way to build a strong foundation of belief is to share God's truths with others. Often, as we share we are asked difficult questions and find ourselves challenged by a different set of beliefs. We are then forced to find the answers to those questions and compare those other beliefs with our own, to determine which beliefs are correct, and why. This process helps you build a strong foundation in understanding what you believe and why you believe it. For those who do not share their faith, this foundation will be absent. We may study as much as we desire, but if we do not gain the experience of defending our faith by answering difficult questions correctly and convincingly through God's guidance, we will not have a strong foundation of belief and will find it hard to defend our faith as we approach the end of this world. The Holy Spirit does not then transform our understanding of our beliefs. We must already have this foundation of understanding what we believe and why we believe it. The Spirit will then help us recall the experiences of the past, and the answers and the texts necessary, and help us to present that information in a more dynamic and convincing way. He does not suddenly give us the understanding of our beliefs that is necessary for answering difficult questions. We must gain an understanding of our beliefs through an experience with Jesus in sharing the gospel with others by sharing the gospel now! This experience will give us the foundation necessary for the Holy Spirit to use us in a dramatic way through the Latter Rain experience.

The Spirit of Prophecy places a very strong emphasis on this principle. It is important for us to be building a strong foundation of our beliefs through the sharing of God's truth to others. For example, do you know what the Scriptural answer is to the teaching of the Secret Rapture or the Seven Year Tribulation? Do you know what the Seven Year Tribulation is, and why it is incorrect? What about the State of the Dead? Do you know the answer to the text quoted in Luke 23:43 that is used to prove that Jesus was in heaven with the thief on the cross on the day that He died? Do you know how to share the Three Angels' Messages? Do you know the difference between Post-millennialism and Pre-millennialism? Friend, we are just scratching the surface of the subjects from which a number of questions could be hurled at you when you are called to defend your faith as we approach the end of this world. Do you know what beliefs are correct and why they are correct? This you will learn as you share with other individuals. Then, when we come to the Little Time of Trouble, the Holy Spirit will be able to use you in a mighty way to help others to understand the truth as it is in Jesus and to understand the Final Events and what is happening around them. They will also come to understand why the belief they held for so long is incorrect.

All we need to do is go share, and Jesus will teach us the answers to the questions and objections that are hurled at us. This prepares us for the reception of the Latter Rain. In addition, sharing the gospel has an even greater benefit. We come closer and closer to Jesus Christ! Our faith grows by leaps and bounds as we pray with the individuals we study with and pray for them as they seek to overcome sin in their lives. We must totally depend on the Lord for their conversion and for victory over the sin that besets them. Because of this dependence on our Lord we draw closer and closer to Him. Our relationship with Him grows in an unprecedented way. As was stated earlier, when we teach the Bible to another individual, we retain up to ninety percent of what is taught. As a result, the Holy Spirit has a lot more Scripture in our minds and hearts to change us to be more like Jesus, and to direct our paths each day.

In addition, it is said that service for other individuals is the key to deep-down internal happiness. The ultimate service we can provide for another individual is introducing him or her to Jesus Christ!

If we have been diligent in studying the Word of God, in giving Bible studies to others, in searching the Scriptures to find the answers to questions and objections, therefore have stored those Scriptures and answers in our hearts and minds, and as a result, when on trial have successfully defended our faith, by God's grace, then when we are cross-examined for our faith we are told in *Our High Calling*, p. 356, *"The servants of Christ are to prepare no set speech to present when brought to trial for their faith. Their preparation is to be made day by day, in treasuring up in their hearts the precious truths of God's Word, in feeding upon the teaching of Christ, and through prayer strengthening their faith"*. If we are prepared, we will easily be able to defend our faith with God's assistance.

However, in *Counsels on Sabbath School Work*, p. 41, mention of the above passage is followed by the warning, *"But if they neglect to fill their minds with the gems of truth, if they do not acquaint themselves with the words of Christ, if they have never tasted the power of His grace in trial, then they cannot expect that the Holy Spirit will bring His words to their remembrance. They are to serve God daily with their undivided affections, and then trust Him."* May each of us serve our Lord by sharing Him with other people, on a regular basis, which will help prepare us for the Latter Rain and the end of this world.

We will conclude this section by continuing on in *Our High Calling*, p. 356. *"You are now to get ready for the time of trial. Now you are to know whether your feet are planted on the Eternal Rock. You must have an individual experience, and not depend upon others for your light. When you are brought to the test, how do you know that you will not be alone, with no earthly friend at your side? Will you then be able to realize that Christ is your support?"* The time to prepare for the Latter Rain is now. Let's gain the experience of working side by side with Jesus for the salvation of souls. Let's develop a strong relationship with Him and allow Him to prepare us for these Final Events!

The Shaking

In *Testimonies for the Church*, Vol. 1, p. 181, the Spirit of Prophecy explains the cause of the Shaking. *"I asked the meaning of the shaking I had seen, and was shown that it would be caused by the straight testimony called forth by the counsel of the True Witness to the Laodiceans. This will have its effect upon the heart of the receiver, and will lead him to exalt the standard and pour forth the straight truth. Some will not bear this straight testimony. They will rise up against it, and this will cause a shaking among God's people."* Those who heed the Counsel of the True Witness, arouse from the lukewarm state characterized by the Laodicean Church, develop the close relationship with Jesus Christ by opening their hearts to Him completely, buy of Jesus the gold tried in the fire which is faith and love, allow Him to put on the white raiment which is His righteousness, put on the eye salve in order to discern spiritual things, and have repented from and overcome their sins, will then exalt God's standard and pour forth the straight truth. God's standard to be exalted at this time is the Seventh-day Sabbath. The straight truth to be poured out at this time is the Three Angels' Messages. Conversely, when the straight testimony is given to those who refuse to heed the Counsel of the True Witness, they rise up against it and it causes a shaking among God's people.

In chapter one we found that the 144,000 are sealed before the Shaking. In *Evangelism*, p. 361 is the following statement, which identifies the time period when the Shaking, or sifting, will occur. (The Shaking and sifting are part of the same act and are therefore the same thing. When the items to be sifted are placed in the sifter, the sifter must be shaken to produce the desired results.) *"When the law of God is made void, the church will be sifted by fiery trials, and a larger proportion than we now anticipate will give heed to seducing spirits and doctrines of devils."* The Shaking will occur when the law of God is made void. This is a reference to the enactment of the National Sunday

Law, which catapults us into the Little Time of Trouble. Obviously, the Shaking then occurs during the Little Time of Trouble.

As we are thrust into the Little Time of Trouble, and individuals worldwide are choosing sides in the Sabbath/Sunday conflict, persecution of Sabbath-keepers will increase. *The Great Controversy*, p. 608, comments on this time period. *"As the storm approaches, a large class who have professed faith in the third angel's message, but have not been sanctified through obedience to the truth, abandon their position and join the ranks of the opposition. By uniting with the world and partaking of its spirit, they have come to view matters in nearly the same light; and when the test is brought, they are prepared to choose the easy, popular side."* Notice why people are shaken out of the church at this time. They were not sanctified through obedience to the truth. They did not heed the Counsel of the True Witness and develop a strong relationship with Jesus. They did not spend time with Him, allowing Him to impress God's truths upon their hearts and minds, and thereby denied the work of the Holy Spirit to sanctify them and help them to follow those truths. They spent much of their time with the world and therefore chose the world's side of the conflict.

In contrast to those who are shaken out of the church at this time are those who have developed a strong relationship with Jesus, have submitted their lives to Him, have allowed the Holy Spirit to help them achieve victory over sin, have received the Seal of God, have shared the gospel with others, and therefore know what they believe and why they believe it, and have now received the Latter Rain and are broadcasting the Three Angels' Messages worldwide. What a difference, amen?

Friend, all Jesus wants is that close relationship with each one of us. He loves us so much; He wants to save us no matter what. However, He doesn't force Himself on us. He therefore can't save us if we do not spend the time with Him and allow the work that heaven wants so earnestly to accomplish in our hearts and minds to be completed.

In addition, He wants to work with us for the salvation of souls. Will you submit your life to Him completely today, spend the time with Him and be in His service for others?

Again, speaking of this time period, Ellen White stated in *The Youth Instructor*, Aug. 3, 1893: *"Nothing short of real, genuine faith will survive the strain that will come upon every soul of man in these last days to test and try him. God must be our refuge; we cannot trust in form, profession, ceremony, or position, or think that because we have a name to live, we shall be able to stand in the day of trial. Everything that can be shaken will be shaken, and those things that cannot be shaken by the deceptions and delusions of these last days, will remain. Rivet the soul to the eternal Rock; for in Christ alone there will be safety."* If Jesus is Lord of our lives and we have that close connection with Him, He will be our safety through the Time of Trouble.

In the *Review and Herald*, Dec. 24, 1889, is this statement, *"There will be an army of steadfast believers who will stand as firm as a rock through the last test. But where in that army are those who have been standard-bearers? Where are those whose voices have sounded in proclaiming the truth to the sinning? Some of them are not there. We look for them, but in the time of shaking they have been unable to stand, and have passed over to the enemy's ranks."* They were shaken out of the church!

How are standard-bearers such as these shaken out of the church? Obviously, an erosion of faith has taken place. One of Satan's main activities as we approach the end of this world will be to discourage people from believing in the Spirit of Prophecy. This will cause an erosion of faith that slowly leads to rebellion against God. In *Selected Messages*, Book 1, p. 49, is the following statement. *"The very last deception of Satan will be to make of none effect the testimony of the Spirit of God. 'Where there is no vision, the people perish' (Prov. 29:18). Satan will work ingeniously, in different ways and through different agencies, to unsettle the confidence of God's remnant people in the true testimony."*

This statement is further expanded in *Testimonies for the Church*, Vol. 4, p. 211. *"It is Satan's plan to weaken the faith of God's people in the Testimonies. Next follows skepticism in regard to the vital points of our faith, the pillars of our position, then doubt as to the Holy Scriptures, and then the downward march to perdition. When the Testimonies, which were once believed, are doubted and given up, Satan knows the deceived ones will not stop at this; and he redoubles his efforts till he launches them into open rebellion, which becomes incurable and ends in destruction."* What a shame!

Summary of This Time Period

Let us put this time period in perspective so we can see the full picture. Remember, the 144,000 are sealed by the time we reach the beginning of the Little Time of Trouble, mainly while the National Sunday Law is being agitated. If they are sealed, then what has occurred? Their judgment has taken place and they have been deemed to be saved. However, does this group of people know they have been judged and deemed to be saved? No, they don't!

In addition, there is another group of people in the church who have not allowed Jesus to be Lord of their lives and have not allowed Him to transform them from within. And many of them may not even realize their lack. When we come to the Little Time of Trouble, the vast majority of those who have not been sealed, have not been judged to be saved, and have not spent the time with Jesus to prepare them for this time period, are then shaken out.

Early Writings, p. 271 states, *"Some had been shaken out and left by the way. The careless and indifferent, who did not join with those who prized victory and salvation enough to perseveringly plead and agonize for it, did not obtain it, and they were left behind in darkness, and their places were immediately filled by others taking hold of the truth and coming into the ranks."*

The Spirit of Prophecy gives further detail in *Testimonies for the Church*, Vol. 6, p. 400. *"As trials thicken around us, both separation and unity will be seen in our ranks. Some who are now ready to take up weapons of warfare will in times of real peril make it manifest that they have not built upon the solid rock; they will yield to temptation. Those who have had great light and precious privileges but have not improved them will, under one pretext or another, go out from us."*

What will you do if an earthquake occurs and your house falls down, killing one of your loved ones? If you have not learned to trust Jesus, you will turn your back on Him just as the Israelites did when they came out of Egypt. When the going got tough, what did the Israelites do? They cursed God because they did not have a strong relationship with Him as Moses did. The same scenario will occur in this time period.

In addition, what will you do when the final test concerning the Sabbath/Sunday conflict occurs and you are threatened with imprisonment or death? The Spirit of Prophecy speaks on this topic in *Testimonies for the Church*, Vol. 5, p. 81. *"The time is not far distant when the test will come to every soul. The mark of the beast will be urged upon us. Those who have step by step yielded to worldly demands and conformed to worldly customs will not find it a hard matter to yield to the powers that be, rather than subject themselves to derision, insult, threatened imprisonment, and death. The contest is between the commandments of God and the commandments of men. In this time the gold will be separated from the dross in the church."* We certainly will need a close walk with Jesus to stand during this time period, won't we?

In closing this section, the important thing to remember during this Shaking time period is not to get discouraged, the church will not fall. In *Selected Messages*, Book 2, p. 380 is the following statement. *"The church may appear as about to fall, but it does not fall. It remains, while the sinners in Zion will be sifted out—the chaff separated from the precious wheat. This is a terrible ordeal, but nevertheless it must take place."*

The Coming of Satan and His Evil Angels

In addition to the Shaking, during the Little Time of Trouble, the Coming of Satan will occur. Describing the Second Beast of Revelation, through whom Satan will work as we approach the end of this world, the apostle John says, *"And he doeth great wonders, so that he maketh fire come down from heaven on the earth in the sight of men, And deceiveth them that dwell on the earth by the means of those miracles which he had power to do in the sight of the beast; saying to them that dwell on the earth, that they should make an image to the beast, which had the wound by a sword, and did live"* (Rev. 13:13,14). What does this symbolism mean? This Second Beast of Revelation 13 is known in symbolic Bible prophecy as Apostate Protestantism combined with the United States and all the democratic countries that follow the United States. Apostate Protestantism will do great wonders, even to the point of making fire come down from heaven onto earth in full view of men, as Satan and his evil angels work through this apostate religious power to deceive the whole world. They will influence the Christian world to make an image, an exact replica, of the first beast of Revelation 13, the Roman Catholic Papacy, due to the miracles that are being performed by this apostate power. Many people will be deceived by these miracles, or wonders, performed by Satan and his evil angels as they work through Apostate Protestantism.

The Spirit of Prophecy comments on Satan's miracles in *Selected Messages*, Vol. 2, p. 51. *"We are warned that in the last days he will work with signs and lying wonders. And he will continue these wonders until the close of probation, that he may point to them as evidence that he is an angel of light and not of darkness."* Obviously, from this text, it is clear that Satan and his evil angels come initially prior to the Close of Probation, during the Little Time of Trouble, working with signs and lying wonders to lead people astray.

In *The Great Controversy*, p. 624, the servant of the Lord states, *"Persons will arise pretending to be Christ Himself, and claiming the title and worship which belong to the world's Redeemer. They will perform wonderful miracles of healing and will profess to have revelations from heaven contradicting the testimony of the Scriptures."* This is what Satan has been doing ever since he was thrown out of heaven. He has always tried to influence people to break God's Ten Commandments as he contradicts the Scriptures. This he will do as he works through men during the Little Time of Trouble to try to influence the faithful to turn their backs on Jesus and instead follow him and his evil angels.

In *Selected Messages*, Vol. 2, p. 51 is the following statement: *"It is the lying wonders of the devil that will take the world captive, and he will cause fire to come down from heaven in the sight of men. He is to work miracles; and this wonderful, miracle-working power is to sweep in the whole world."* The entire world will see the miracle-working power of Satan!

The evil angels will appear to us and will work miracles as well, as reported in *Early Writings*, p. 87. *"I saw that the saints must get a thorough understanding of present truth, which they will be obliged to maintain from the Scriptures. They must understand the state of the dead; for the spirits of devils will yet appear to them, professing to be beloved friends and relatives, who will declare to them that the Sabbath has been changed, also other unscriptural doctrines. They will do all in their power to excite sympathy and will work miracles before them to confirm what they declare."* Every time the evil angels declare that the Sabbath was changed, they will work a miracle to convince people to follow them. This will be extremely deceptive to those who do not know what the truth is.

This deception is further described in *Signs of the Times*, Aug. 26, 1889. *"It is Satan's most successful and fascinating delusion,—one calculated to take hold of the sympathies of those who have laid their loved ones in the grave. Evil angels come in the form of those loved ones, and relate incidents connected with their lives, and perform acts which they performed while living. In this way they lead persons to believe that their dead friends are angels, hovering over them, and communicating with them. These evil angels, who assume to be the deceased friends, are regarded with a certain idolatry, and with many their word has greater weight than the word of God. Thus men and women are led to reject the truth, and give 'heed to seducing spirits.' "*

Another description of this deception, with more detail, is found in *The Great Controversy*, pp. 552, 553. *"He has power to bring before men the appearance of their departed friends. The counterfeit is perfect; the familiar look, the words, the tone, are reproduced with marvelous distinctness. Many are comforted with the assurance that their loved ones are enjoying the bliss of heaven, and without suspicion of danger, they give ear to 'seducing spirits, and doctrines of devils.'*

When they have been led to believe that the dead actually return to communicate with them, Satan causes those to appear who went into the grave unprepared. They claim to be happy in heaven and even to occupy exalted positions there, and thus the error is widely taught that no difference is made between the righteous and the wicked. The pretended visitants from the world of spirits sometimes utter cautions and warnings which prove to be correct. Then, as confidence is gained, they present doctrines that directly undermine faith in the Scriptures. With an appearance of deep interest in the well-being of their friends on earth, they insinuate the most dangerous errors. The fact that they state some truths, and are able at times to foretell future events, gives to their statements an appearance of reliability; and their false teachings are accepted by the multitudes as readily, and believed as implicitly, as if they were the most sacred truths of the Bible. The law of God is set aside, the Spirit of grace despised, the blood of the covenant counted an unholy thing. The spirits deny the deity of Christ and place even the Creator on a level with themselves. Thus under a new disguise the great rebel still carries on his warfare against God, begun in heaven and for nearly six thousand years continued upon the earth." Do you see how deceptive this will be? This will be so deceptive it could deceive anyone who is not grounded in biblical truth. This will occur for some during the Little Time of Trouble. However, during the Great Time of Trouble, as the work of Satan and his evil angels intensifies, all of the lost will be deceived by the impersonation of their dead loved ones and friends, and gathered together for the Battle of Armageddon, as we will discover in the next chapter.

Another aspect of the work of the evil angels is described in *Selected Messages*, Vol. 3, p. 410. *"I have been shown that evil angels in the form of believers will work in our ranks to bring in a strong spirit of unbelief. Let not even this discourage you, but bring a true heart to the help of the Lord against the powers of satanic agencies.*

These powers of evil will assemble in our meetings, not to receive a blessing, but to counterwork the influences of the Spirit of God.... Christ was the Instructor in the assemblies of these angels before they fell from their high estate." These evil angels will be present with us in the form of human beings, to counteract the Holy Spirit's influence. Imagine that!

They will also be present with us when they impersonate the apostles. In *The Great Controversy*, p. 557, is the following comment. *"The apostles, as personated by these lying spirits, are made to contradict what they wrote at the dictation of the Holy Spirit when on earth. They deny the divine origin of the Bible."* Imagine that! The apostles, Peter, James, John, Paul, Matthew, Mark, and Luke, as impersonated by evil angels, deny the divine origin of their own writings in the New Testament!

Then Satan himself will appear as he impersonates Jesus. *Testimonies to Ministers and Gospel Workers*, p. 411 states, *"The conflict is to wax fiercer and fiercer. Satan will take the field and personate Christ. He will misrepresent, misapply, and pervert everything he possibly can, to deceive, if possible, the very elect."*

The counterfeit of Jesus will be so deceptive that those who do not know the biblical teaching of the Second Coming of Christ, that Jesus will not touch this earth but will remain in the cloud in the air, will easily be deceived. In *Fundamentals of Christian Education*, pp. 471, 472, the servant of the Lord describes this deceit. *"Disguised as an angel of light, he will walk the earth as a wonder-worker. In beautiful language he will present lofty sentiments. Good words will be spoken by him, and good deeds performed. Christ will be personified, but on one point there will be a marked distinction. Satan will turn the people from the law of God. Notwithstanding this, so well will he counterfeit righteousness, that if it were possible, he would deceive the very elect. Crowned heads, presidents, rulers in high places, will bow to his false theories."* Satan will be so deceptive as we approach the end of this world, that well-meaning Christians that are not close to Jesus Christ will easily be deceived.

In *Last Day Events*, p. 164, this deception is further explained. *"He proclaims himself Christ, and he is believed to be Christ, a beautiful, majestic being clothed with majesty and, with soft voice and pleasant words, with glory unsurpassed by anything their mortal eyes had yet beheld. Then his deceived, deluded followers set up a shout of victory, "Christ has come the second time! Christ has come! He has lifted up His hands just as He did when He was upon the earth, and blessed us."* Imagine that! These people believe that Jesus has come and that they are being blessed by Jesus, when it is Satan himself who "blesses" them! What a deceptive time we have coming when we enter the Time of Trouble!

The Coming of Satan is summarized in *The Great Controversy*, pp. 624, 625 as follows: *"As the crowning act in the great drama of deception, Satan himself will personate Christ. The church has long professed to look to the Saviour's advent as the consummation of her hopes. Now the great deceiver will make it appear that Christ has come. In different parts of the earth, Satan will manifest himself among men as a majestic being of dazzling brightness, resembling the description of the Son of God given by John in the Revelation. Revelation*

1:13-15. The glory that surrounds him is unsurpassed by anything that mortal eyes have yet beheld. The shout of triumph rings out upon the air: 'Christ has come! Christ has come!' The people prostrate themselves in adoration before him, while he lifts up his hands and pronounces a blessing upon them, as Christ blessed His disciples when He was upon the earth. His voice is soft and subdued, yet full of melody. In gentle, compassionate tones he presents some of the same gracious, heavenly truths which the Saviour uttered; he heals the diseases of the people, and then, in his assumed character of Christ, he claims to have changed the Sabbath to Sunday, and commands all to hallow the day which he has blessed. He declares that those who persist in keeping holy the seventh day are blaspheming his name by refusing to listen to his angels sent to them with light and truth. This is the strong, almost overmastering delusion. Like the Samaritans who were deceived by Simon Magus, the multitudes, from the least to the greatest, give heed to these sorceries, saying: This is 'the great power of God.'" Acts 8:10. They believe it is the great power of God when it is, in fact, the power of Satan. Imagine that!

Now friend, while we learned earlier that Satan and his evil angels will work during the Little Time of Trouble, with signs and lying wonders, until the Close of Probation, and have explored several ways in which they will work, this last mode of deception, Satan's impersonation of Christ, the Spirit of Prophecy seems to indicate will occur as Satan's work intensifies and we pass into the Great Time of Trouble. Please keep this in mind.

The Spirit of Prophecy gives us some encouragement for this time period in *The Great Controversy*, p. 560. *"Just before us is 'the hour of temptation, which shall come upon all the world, to try them that dwell upon the earth.' Revelation 3:10. All whose faith is not firmly established upon the word of God will be deceived and overcome. Satan 'works with all deceivableness of unrighteousness' to gain control of the children of men, and his deceptions will continually increase. But he can gain his object only as men voluntarily yield to his temptations. Those who are earnestly seeking a knowledge of the truth and are striving to purify their souls through obedience, thus doing what they can to prepare for the conflict, will find, in the God of truth, a sure defense. 'Because thou hast kept the word of my patience, I also will keep thee' (verse 10), is the Saviour's promise. He would sooner send every angel out of heaven to protect His people than leave one soul that trusts in Him to be overcome by Satan."* Amen.

The Second Sunday Law

Due to the deception of Satan and his evil angels during the Little Time of Trouble, they will have gathered a multitude of people on their side, including the world's governments controlled by Apostate Protestantism. These governments then pronounce a Second Sunday Law as described in Revelation 13:16, 17. *"And he causeth all, both small and great, rich and poor, free and bond, to receive a mark in their right hand, or in their foreheads: And that no man might buy or sell, save he that had the mark, or the name of the beast, or the number of his name."* Apostate Protestantism, as it works through the world's governments, causes those who are lost to receive a physical mark that comes as a result of the spiritual mark that has been accepted into their minds and in their hearts to defy heaven by breaking the Ten Commandments and following the Venerable Day of the Sun, as promoted by Satan and his evil angels. When this Second Sunday Law occurs, no one will be able to buy or sell unless they have the mark of the papal power or they have the name of the beast, meaning they are part of the Roman Catholic Papacy, or they have the number of his name, which would be the pope himself.

The Spirit of Prophecy comments on the state of affairs for those who oppose the Second Sunday Law, in *Maranatha*, p. 209, *"I saw our people in great distress, weeping, and praying, pleading the sure promises of God, while the wicked were all around us, mocking us, and threatening to destroy us. They ridiculed our feebleness, they mocked at the smallness of our numbers, and taunted us with words calculated to cut deep. They charged us with taking an independent position from all the rest of the world. They had cut off our resources so that we could not buy nor sell, and referred to our abject poverty and stricken condition. They could not see how we could live without the world; we were dependent upon the world, and we must concede to the customs, practices, and laws of the world, or go out of it. If we were the only people in the world whom the Lord favored the appearances were awfully against us. They declared that they had the truth, that miracles were among them, that angels from heaven talked with them, and walked with them, that great power, and signs and wonders were performed among them, and this was the Temporal Millennium, which they had been expecting so long. The whole world was converted and in harmony with the Sunday law, and this little feeble people stood out in defiance of the laws of the land, and the laws of God, and claimed to be the only ones right on the earth."* At this time we will have our loved ones saying, "what, are you crazy? You're not going to eat! You have no food! You can't buy or sell! Look at the appearance. You cannot be the ones who are right! All of us are blessed! We have talked and walked with angels! Miracles have been performed amongst us! We have the truth!" At this time God's people will appear poverty-stricken while the rest of the world seems blessed.

Also, they will point to this time period as the Temporal Millennium, the thousand years of peace. According to Post-millennial theology, the church will come into power at the beginning of the millennium here on planet earth and rule for a thousand years, and then Jesus comes. This belief is promoted by Pat Robertson and other evangelicals. This is why False Christianity wants to combine church with state, which will have taken place at this time. In the Little Time of Trouble they will believe they have entered the Millennium, because False Christianity is ruling the world. They then point to God's true people and say "how can they be right"? The sad fact is that if the Bible were understood correctly, they would find that the Millennium does not occur until after the Second Coming of Christ, a time in which God's people are taken to heaven for the thousand years, and do not remain here on planet earth during the Millennium!

This time period reminds me of the text in 1 Thessalonians 5:3, "For when they shall say, Peace and safety; then sudden destruction cometh upon them, as travail upon a woman with child; and they shall not escape." During the Little Time of Trouble False Christianity proclaims this belief of a thousand years of peace and safety. However, a short time later they receive the Seven Last Plagues of the Great Time of Trouble. The proclamation of peace and safety will certainly be followed by sudden destruction, just as the Bible has predicted.

The Final Sealing Before the Four Winds Are Released

As we near the end of the Little Time of Trouble, all of God's people, the final 144000, must be sealed. This will take place before the winds are released to start the Great Time of Trouble, when probation will have closed. Jesus will see to it that anyone who is to be saved will be sealed prior to the Close of Probation as a Point in Time. In *Early Writings*, p. 38, is the following: *"I saw four angels who had a work to do on the earth, and were on their way to accomplish it. Jesus was clothed with priestly garments. He gazed in pity on the remnant, then raised His hands, and with a voice of deep pity cried, "My blood, Father, My blood, My blood, My blood!" Then I saw an exceeding bright light come from God, who sat upon the great white throne, and was shed all about Jesus. Then I saw an angel with a commission from Jesus, swiftly flying to the four angels who had a work to do on the earth, and waving something up and down in his hand, and crying with a loud voice, "Hold! Hold! Hold! Hold! until the servants of God are sealed in their foreheads.*

I asked my accompanying angel the meaning of what I heard, and what the four angels were about to do. He said to me that it was God that restrained the powers, and that He gave His angels charge over things on the earth; that the four angels had power from God to hold the four winds, and that they were about to let them go; but while their hands were loosening, and the four winds were about to blow, the merciful eye of Jesus gazed on the remnant that were not sealed, and He raised His hands to the Father and pleaded with Him that He had spilled His blood for them. Then another angel was commissioned to fly swiftly to the four angels and bid them hold, until the servants of God were sealed with the seal of the living God in their foreheads." Amen.

How Do We Stand Against Satan and His Evil Angels During the Little Time of Trouble?

As we contemplate this period of the Little Time of Trouble, and realize that Satan and his evil angels will come and deceive millions of people here on earth, how do we stand against Satan and his evil angels during this time period?

The Lord gives us the answer to this question in Ephesians 6:10-18. *"Finally, my brethren, be strong in the Lord, and in the power of his might. Put on the whole armour of God, that ye may be able to stand against the wiles of the devil. For we wrestle not against flesh and blood, but against principalities, against powers, against the rulers of the darkness of this world, against spiritual wickedness in high places. Wherefore take unto you the whole armour of God, that ye may be able to withstand in the evil day, and having done all, to stand."* How do we stand against Satan and his evil angels during the Little Time of Trouble? By putting on the armour of God!

"Stand therefore, having your loins girt about with truth". What is the truth? Where is it found? It is found in God's Word, the Bible, of course. We must put on God's Word. We must allow the Holy Spirit to impress God's Word upon our minds and hearts thereby allowing God to change us to be like Jesus, to reflect His Word in our lives.

". . . and having on the breastplate of righteousness." Where does righteousness come from? From Jesus, of course! As we allow Jesus into our lives and surrender to Him, the Holy Spirit works upon our hearts and minds to change us and to put on us the righteousness of Jesus Christ!

"And your feet shod with the preparation of the gospel of peace." What is the gospel? The good news, the Word of God! Again, we are to put on the Word of God through our relationship with Jesus, as we allow Him to talk to us through His Word, as we accept His Word into our hearts and minds, and, under the guidance of the Holy Spirit, follow His Word.

"Above all, taking the shield of faith, wherewith ye shall be able to quench all the fiery darts of the wicked." How do we take the shield of faith? "So then faith cometh by hearing, and hearing by the word of God" (Rom. 10:17). Obviously, faith comes by studying the Word of God. This is how we take the shield of faith! Again, the emphasis is on the relationship with Jesus Christ.

"And take the helmet of salvation and the sword of the Spirit, which is the word of God." This is the fourth reference to the armor of God being the Word of God. The whole armor of God is God's Word and

Jesus' righteousness being brought into our minds and our hearts. We must put on Jesus and His Word.

Throughout this book we have seen that this is the main message we are given in the Spirit of Prophecy and in the Scripture, that we must bring Jesus and His Word into our minds and hearts on a daily basis. Everything revolves around our relationship with Jesus. We must have the close relationship with Jesus. This is the preparation necessary for these Final Events and the end of the world.

Sadly, as mentioned earlier, according to surveys, a large percentage of Seventh-day Adventists do not have a daily relationship with Jesus!

Paul mentions one more element that must be present as we put on the armor of God. *"Praying always with all prayer and supplication in the Spirit, and watching thereunto with all perseverance and supplication for all saints."* To be prepared for these Final Events we must have an active prayer life. Unfortunately, according to a survey conducted in the year 2001, many of us do not have an active prayer life. In this survey the question was asked whether or not the participants had prayed to God in the last seven days. Constituents of twelve different denominations took part in this survey. Pentecostals topped the list, with 97% of those surveyed answering yes to this question. The national average for this survey was 82%. However, Seventh-day Adventists were last among the twelve denominations, with 79% answering yes.[6] Friend, if you are among those who do not have a daily relationship with Jesus, are not talking to Him in prayer, and are not allowing Him to talk to you through the study of His Word, I encourage you strongly to begin this relationship with Him today. He will change your life and prepare you for heaven!

Remember, prayer plus putting on the armor of God (God's Word, the righteousness of Jesus) is the protection necessary to stand up against Satan and his evil angels and see us through the Little Time of Trouble, the Great Time of Trouble, and the Second Coming of Jesus Christ!

Chapter 5

The Great Time of Trouble: the Seven Last Plagues, the Third Sunday Law, and the Time of Jacob's Trouble

A s individuals throughout the world make their final decision during the Little Time of Trouble and have either settled into the truth, or into the error, their judgment takes place in recognition of that decision, and they receive the Seal of God or the Mark of the Beast. When every person on earth has made their decision, the judgment is concluded, the Close of Probation as a Point in Time occurs, and we then find ourselves in the Great Time of Trouble.

As revealed in Chapter One, Daniel 12:1 summarizes the Great Time of Trouble. *"And at that time shall Michael stand up, the great prince which standeth for the children of thy people: and there shall be a time of trouble, such as never was since there was a nation even to that same time: and at that time thy people shall be delivered, every one that shall be found written in the book."* When Jesus stands up, what has occurred? The judgment has concluded and probation is closed. The Bible says we are then thrown into *"a time of trouble, such as never was,"* the Great Time of Trouble. *"And at that time thy people shall be delivered, every one that shall be found written in the book."* When the Great Time of Trouble occurs, all those who are written in the Book of Life are delivered from this time of trouble by Jesus at His

Second Coming. These events can be seen on your chart from the third vertical line to the fourth vertical line.

As we consider the Great Time of Trouble, we find that when probation closes the Holy Spirit is withdrawn from those who are lost. The details of this withdrawal are revealed in *The Great Controversy*, pp. 613, 614. *"When He leaves the sanctuary, darkness covers the inhabitants of the earth. In that fearful time the righteous must live in the sight of a holy God without an intercessor. The restraint which has been upon the wicked is removed, and Satan has entire control of the finally impenitent. God's long-suffering has ended. The world has rejected His mercy, despised His love, and trampled upon His law. The wicked have passed the boundary of their probation; the Spirit of God, persistently resisted, has been at last withdrawn. Unsheltered by divine grace, they have no protection from the wicked one. Satan will then plunge the inhabitants of the earth into one great, final trouble. As the angels of God cease to hold in check the fierce winds of human passion, all the elements of strife will be let loose."* After probation closes, Satan plunges us into one great final trouble as the Lord releases the winds.

The Seven Last Plagues

The time period when the Seven Last Plagues will be poured out is addressed in *Early Writings*, p. 36. *"When our High Priest has finished His work in the sanctuary, He will stand up, put on the garments of vengeance, and then the seven last plagues will be poured out."* As revealed in the last two quotations, the winds are released and consequently the Seven Last Plagues are poured out after Jesus has completed the judgment, and probation is closed. Therefore this event is located in your chart under the Great Time of Trouble.

The Spirit of Prophecy describes the initial plagues in *The Great Controversy*, pp. 628, 629. *"These [first four] plagues are not universal, or the inhabitants of the earth would be wholly cut off. Yet they will be the most awful scourges that have ever been known to mortals. All the judgments upon men, prior to the close of probation, have been mingled with mercy. . . . , but in the final Judgment, wrath is poured out unmixed with mercy.*

In that day, multitudes will desire the shelter of God's mercy which they have so long despised." As we can see, the first four plagues are not universal. If they were, every human being would be killed by them! Instead, they are regional plagues that wreak havoc more than any prior judgment.

Also, as revealed earlier, the judgments that fall during the Little Time of Trouble are mixed with mercy while the judgments that fall during the Great Time of Trouble under the Seven Last Plagues are un-mixed with mercy.

During this time period, God's people will not initially know that probation has closed. How will God's people begin to suspect that pro-bation has closed? When the outpouring of the Seven Last Plagues oc-curs, due to the fact the outpouring of the plagues is the first event that occurs after probation closes.

As we begin to study the Seven Last Plagues, we must first deter-mine who receives the plagues and why. Revelation 14:9, 10 states: *"And the third angel followed them, saying with a loud voice, If any man worship the beast and his image, and receive his mark in his fore-head, or in his hand, The same shall drink of the wine of the wrath of God".* We know from this statement that whoever worships the beast, whom we know in symbolic Bible prophecy represents the Roman Catholic Papacy, or his image, whom we know to be Apostate Protes-tantism, and receives the beast's mark in the forehead or in the hand, re-ceived by commitment to and worship on Sunday, instead of God's Sabbath, will then drink of the wine of the wrath of God. The question, then, is what is the wrath of God? Revelation 15:1 provides the answer. *"And I saw another sign in heaven, great and marvellous, seven angels having the seven last plagues; for in them is filled up the wrath of God."* You see, those who are lost and worship the beast and his image and have received the Mark of the Beast will receive the Seven Last Plagues during the Great Time of Trouble, which is the wrath of God.

God informs us of the plagues, beginning in Revelation 16:1,2. *"And I heard a great voice out of the temple saying to the seven angels, Go your ways, and pour out the vials of the wrath of God upon the earth. And the first went, and poured out his vial upon the earth; and there fell a noisome and grievous sore upon the men which had the mark of the beast, and upon them which worshipped his image."* Those who have the Mark of the Beast, or worship the beast's image, Apostate Protestantism, receive the first plague, a sore that comes upon each of them. It is at this time that those who are saved and know the Scriptures will then realize that the judgment has passed and probation is closed.

Testimonies, Vol. 1, p. 204 states, *"When Jesus leaves the most holy, His restraining Spirit is withdrawn from rulers and people. They are left to the control of evil angels. Then such laws will be made by the counsel and direction of Satan, that unless time should be very short, no flesh could be saved."* Once the judgment has been completed and the Holy Spirit is withdrawn, the rulers on earth, led by Satan and his evil angels as they work through Apostate Protestantism, enact the Third Sunday Law, a law established to kill every saint on earth who will not observe the Sun's day and worship on the Venerable Day of the Sun, thereby receiving the Mark of the Beast.

The Third Sunday Law

This law and the fate of those who are condemned by it are described in Revelation 13:15. *"And he had power to give life unto the image of the beast, that the image of the beast should both speak, and cause that as many as would not worship the image of the beast should be killed."* Once again, who is the image of the beast? Apostate Protestantism, of course! Apostate Protestantism will force the world to follow its brand of worship, an image of the worship of Papal Rome, which has at the forefront the observance of the Venerable Day of the Sun, or be killed, through the enactment of a Third Sunday Law.

We receive a complete picture of this time period from *Testimonies,* Vol. 5, pp. 212, 213. *"When this time of trouble comes, every case is decided; there is no longer probation, no longer mercy for the impenitent. The seal of the living God is upon His people. This small remnant, unable to defend themselves in the deadly conflict with the powers of earth that are marshaled by the dragon host, make God their defense. The decree has been passed by the highest earthly authority that they shall worship the beast and receive his mark under pain of persecution and death. May God help His people now, for what can they do in such a fearful conflict without His assistance."* During this time period, when the final Sunday Law is passed, a law that insists that we receive and follow the Mark of the Beast, the observance of the Venerable Day of the Sun, or be killed, God's people must have come to a place in their experience of total trust in Him, which will enable them to go through the Great Time of Trouble and stand up for Jesus Christ. Remember, as we learned in Chapter 3, it is the Latter Rain that prepares the saints to stand in this period when the Seven Last Plagues are poured out.

Early Writings, pp. 36, 37 states, *"I saw that the four angels would hold the four winds until Jesus' work was done in the sanctuary, and then will come the seven last plagues. These plagues enraged the wicked against the righteous; they thought that we had brought the judgments of God upon them, and that if they could rid the earth of us, the plagues would then be stayed. A decree went forth to slay the saints, which caused them to cry day and night for deliverance. This was the time of Jacob's trouble."* When this Third Sunday Law is issued, a decree to kill all of God's people at a certain time, we are then thrown into what is called the Time of Jacob's Trouble, which you will find in the middle of your chart located under the Great Time of Trouble.

God has given us an example of what occurs at this time in history from the time of Elijah. In Elijah's time it hadn't rained for three and one half years. This was a plague wasn't it? And Elijah was standing up for God and His Ten Commandments. Elijah had prayed that it wouldn't rain for three and one half years because the sun worshippers believed that Baal, the sun or weather god, controlled the sun and the rain. Elijah was a faithful follower of the Lord and he later stood for the Lord on Mount Carmel against four hundred and fifty prophets of Baal.

Just prior to the conflict on Mount Carmel, Ahab, the king of Israel, and an advocate of sun worship, came to Elijah. The conversation that followed is recorded in 1 Kings 18:17, 18. *"And it came to pass, when Ahab saw Elijah, that Ahab said unto him, Art thou he that troubleth Israel?"* You see, Ahab believed that Elijah was the cause of the plague and, therefore, responsible for Israel's trouble.

Elijah responded by saying, *"I have not troubled Israel; but thou, and thy father's house, in that ye have forsaken the commandments of the Lord, and thou hast followed Baalim."* The king and the people of his country believed that Elijah was the cause of the plague. But who was really responsible? They were! They had forsaken God's Ten Commandments and were worshipping the sun god Baal. This is the real reason the plague came upon them.

The same situation will occur as we approach the end of this world. God's people, who are following all of the Ten Commandments, will be blamed for the first plague. The leaders of this planet and all of their people will point the finger at God's true people, insisting that because we refuse to follow the world's Sunday laws God is unhappy with this planet and thus has given us this plague. In reality though, the blame falls on all those who worship on Sunday and have forsaken the commandments of the Lord. In Elijah's time the people forsook the commandments of the Lord and worshipped the Sun God Baal, and therefore received the plague. In our time, the people have forsaken the commandments of the Lord and worshipped on the Sun God's day, Sunday, and therefore will receive the plagues.

As the blame falls on God's true people, those who follow all of His Ten Commandments, the Third Sunday Law is passed, as described in detail in the *Story of Redemption*, p. 406. *"I saw the leading men of the earth consulting together, and Satan and his angels busy around them. I saw a writing, copies of which were scattered in different parts of the land, giving orders that unless the saints should yield their peculiar faith, give up the Sabbath, and observe the first day of the week, the people were at liberty after a certain time to put them to death."* The decree comes forth after the first plague, which gives them liberty after a certain amount of time, probably on a particular day at midnight, to put God's people to death.

The biblical example of this death decree is found in the story of Esther. All of the Jews were to be put to death after a certain amount of time, as recorded in Esther 3:13. *"And the letters were sent by posts into all the king's provinces, to destroy, to kill, and to cause to perish, all Jews, both young and old, little children and women, in one day, even upon the thirteenth day of the twelfth month, which is the month Adar, and to take the spoil of them for a prey."* As the day approached, God rescued His people through His servant, Queen Esther.

As we approach the end of this world and the day of this death decree approaches, God's people will be rescued by their king, Jesus Christ, at His Second Coming, as we will discover shortly.

This time period is described in *The Great Controversy*, p. 615 as follows. *"It will be urged that the few who stand in opposition to an institution of the church and a law of the state ought not to be tolerated; that it is better for them to suffer than for whole nations to be thrown into confusion and lawlessness. The same argument eighteen hundred years ago was brought against Christ by the 'rulers of the people.' 'It is expedient for us,' said the wily Caiaphas, 'that one man should die for the people, and that the whole nation perish not.' John 11:50. This argument will appear conclusive; and a decree will finally be issued against those who hallow the Sabbath of the fourth commandment, denouncing them as deserving of the severest punishment and giving the people liberty, after a certain time, to put them to death."*

After receiving the first plague, the world's governments, as controlled by False Christianity, pass a death decree, the Third Sunday Law. It permits the people of the world to put God's people, those who follow the Ten Commandments, to death after a certain time. The Lord responds to this death decree against His people with the second and third plagues.

These plagues are described in Revelation 16:3-7. *"And the second angel poured out his vial upon the sea; and it became as the blood of a dead man: and every living soul died in the sea. And the third angel poured out his vial upon the rivers and fountains of waters; and they became blood. And I heard the angel of the waters say, Thou art righteous, O Lord, which art, and wast, and shalt be, because thou hast judged thus. For they have shed the blood of saints and prophets, and thou hast given them blood to drink; for they are worthy. And I heard another out of the altar say, Even so, Lord God Almighty, true and righteous are thy judgments."* Why is False Christianity given blood to drink? Because during the dark ages, it is estimated, the Roman Catholic Papacy killed fifty million Christians.[7] During the Little Time of Trouble, Apostate Protestantism and the Roman Catholic Papacy will persecute and kill many more of God's people. During the Great Time of Trouble, Apostate Christianity will pass a death decree to kill all of God's remaining people. The Lord then responds with the plagues of blood, as they are given blood to drink.

The Spirit of Prophecy describes this time period in *The Great Controversy*, p. 628, as follows. *"Terrible as these inflictions are, God's justice stands fully vindicated. The angel of God declares: 'Thou art righteous, O Lord ....because Thou hast judged thus. For they have shed the blood of saints and prophets, and Thou hast given them blood to drink; for they are worthy.' Revelation 16:2-6. By condemning the people of God to death, they have as truly incurred the guilt of their blood as if it had been shed by their hands."* Remember, as revealed previously, these plagues are poured out, turning the seas and rivers into blood in regional parts of the world. With modern technology the salt water of the seas can be changed into fresh drinking water through distillation, reverse osmosis, or electrolysis. However, in those regions where the seas as well as rivers have turned to blood, there is no way to obtain drinking water. They have all been given blood to drink.

The Great Controversy, p. 635, states, *"When the protection of human laws shall be withdrawn from those who honor the law of God, there will be, in different lands, a simultaneous movement for their destruction. As the time appointed in the decree draws near, the people will conspire to root out the hated sect. It will be determined to strike in one night a decisive blow, which shall utterly silence the voice of dissent and reproof."*

The governments of this world, as led by False Christianity, determine at a particular night to kill all of God's people. This terrible decree tosses God's true people into a time period previously named in *Early Writings*, pp. 36, 37, as follows: *"A decree went forth to slay the saints, which caused them to cry day and night for deliverance. This was the time of Jacob's trouble."*

The Time of Jacob's Trouble

The pain and anguish of the Time of Jacob's Trouble is described in Jeremiah 30:5-7. *"For thus saith the Lord; We have heard a voice of trembling, of fear, and not of peace. Ask ye now, and see whether a man doth travail with child? wherefore do I see every man with his hands on his loins, as a woman in travail, and all faces are turned into paleness? Alas! for that day is great , so that none is like it: it is even the time of Jacob's trouble; but he shall be saved out of it."* This text describes the Time of Jacob's Trouble as causing so much pain and anguish it is compared with a man giving birth to a child. This is a pain and anguish so intense it has never been felt before by a man. This is a time period never seen before on planet earth.

The original Time of Jacob's Trouble is described in Genesis 32:24-30. *"And Jacob was left alone; and there wrestled a man with him until the breaking of the day. And when he saw that he prevailed not against him, he touched the hollow of his thigh; and the hollow of Jacob's thigh was out of joint, as he wrestled with him. And he said, Let me go, for the day breaketh. And he said, I will not let thee go, except thou bless me. And he said unto him, What is thy name? And he said, Jacob. And he said, Thy name shall be called no more Jacob, but Israel: for as a prince hast thou power with God and with men, and hast prevailed. And Jacob asked him, and said, Tell me, I pray thee, thy name. And he said, Wherefore is it that thou dost ask after my name? And he blessed him there. And Jacob called the name of the place Peniel: for I have seen God face to face, and my life is preserved."* Jacob sees the Lord face to face as he wrestles with God all night and tells the Lord he would not let Him go until He blessed him. This will be the experience of those who come up to this time period just before Jesus' return, are facing the death penalty, and are in complete anguish. They will be wrestling with God all night in prayer and will not let Him go until they receive the blessing and assurance of being saved and delivered from their enemies.

This stretch of time is described in *Spiritual Gifts*, Vol. 3, pp.131, 132. *"Jacob and Esau represent two classes; Jacob, the righteous, and Esau the wicked. Jacob's distress when he learned that Esau was marching against him with four hundred men, represents the trouble of the righteous as the decree goes forth to put them to death, just before the coming of the Lord. As the wicked gather about them they will be filled with anguish, for like Jacob they can see no escape for their lives. The angel placed himself before Jacob, and he took hold of the angel and held him, and wrestled with him all night. So also will the righteous, in their time of trouble and anguish, wrestle in prayer with God, as Jacob wrestled with the angel. Jacob in his distress prayed all night for deliverance from the hand of Esau. The righteous in their mental anguish will cry to God day and night for deliverance from the hand of the wicked who surround them."* This will be an awful time for God's people!

The Spirit of Prophecy further describes this time period as a time of testing, in *Signs of the Times*, Nov. 27, 1879. *"In these days of peril [the Great Time of Trouble] those who have been unfaithful in their duties in life, and whose mistakes and sins of neglect are registered against them in the book in Heaven, unrepented of and unforgiven, will be overcome by Satan . . . These will have no shelter in the time of Jacob's trouble. Their sins will then appear of such magnitude that they will have no confidence to pray, no heart to wrestle as did Jacob. On the other hand, those who have been of like passion, erring and sinful in their lives, but who have repented of their sins, and in genuine sorrow confessed them, will have pardon written against their names in the heavenly records. They will be hid in the day of the Lord's anger. Satan will attack this class, but like Jacob they have taken hold of the strength of God, and true to his character he is at peace with them, and sends angels to comfort and bless and sustain them in their time of peril. The time of Jacob's trouble will test every one, and distinguish the genuine Christian from the one who is so only in name."* Since this is a testing time, a question that comes immediately to my mind and probably to yours is, why would God test His people after the Close of Probation? The judgment has been completed at this time. Every case has been decided. Why would God test us at this time? The answer to this question will be seen by combining this quotation with the next several Spirit of Prophecy passages.

We will begin with a description of this time period found in *The Great Controversy*, p. 620. *"Had not Jacob previously repented of his sin in obtaining the birthright by fraud, God would not have heard his prayer and mercifully preserved his life. So, in the time of trouble, if the people of God had unconfessed sins to appear before them while tortured with fear and anguish, they would be overwhelmed; despair would cut off their faith, and they could not have confidence to plead with God for deliverance. But while they have a deep sense of their unworthiness, they have no concealed wrongs to reveal. Their sins have*

*gone beforehand to judgment and have been blotted out, and they can-
not bring them to remembrance."* What a blessing that will be! Our sins
cannot be recalled!

The Spirit of Prophecy gives further detail concerning this forget-
fulness in *Spiritual Gifts*, Vol. 3, pp. 134, 135. *"The righteous will not
cease their earnest agonizing cries for deliverance. They cannot bring
to mind any particular sins, but in their whole life they can see but little good. Their sins had gone beforehand to judgment, and pardon had
been written. Their sins had been borne away into the land of forgetful-
ness, and they could not bring them to remembrance."* Miraculously,
our past sins can no longer be remembered!

While the righteous have confessed and repented of their sins and
are no longer able to recall them, we can understand from these last
few passages that, apparently, there will be a group of people that has
gone through the Little Time of Trouble and has not confessed and repented of all their sins, but has not yet been shaken out of God's
church! These people will be those who did not have a real close relationship with Jesus, did not therefore repent of all their sins, but remained strong enough to stay in the church through the Little Time of
Trouble, probably due to their relationship to another Christian. For example, the brother of a pastor who is strong because of his pastor
brother but is not strong himself, and has not really surrendered his life
to Jesus Christ. In the Great Time of Trouble, these individuals become
horrified because they have not confessed and forsaken all of their sins.
They therefore are overwhelmed by this fact, and the despair cuts off
their faith.

Brother or sister in Christ, we must have a close relationship with
Jesus, confess and forsake all of our sins, allow Jesus to help us overcome sin in our lives, and leave everything else to Jesus in the judgment. God is not going to close probation until each Christian is ready.
God will wait until every Christian who is willing to settle into the
truth does so before He closes their probation. Prior to the Great Time
of Trouble, God will bring all of our sins to our remembrance and we
must confess them and forsake them. As long as we are willing to, He
will not close our probation until this is accomplished. God wants to
save every human being He can possibly save.

On the other hand, the wheat and the tares will grow together in God's church until the harvest, or the Second Coming of Christ. The majority of the tares will be shaken out during the Little Time of Trouble. However there will be a few left when we enter the Great Time of Trouble. The person to whom God brings remembrance of his or her sins but does not confess and forsake them, will come into the Great Time of Trouble, will be overwhelmed, and will cut himself or herself off. What a shame that will be for these individuals.

How Will We Survive?

As we go through the latter stages of the Little Time of Trouble, and go through the Great Time of Trouble and come up to the Time of Jacob's Trouble, the question that always comes to mind is, how are we going to make it? We can't buy or sell! How are we going to endure this period of time? Will we starve? Should we store up food? Let's allow the servant of the Lord to answer this last question first, as she does so in *Early Writings*, p. 56. *"The Lord has shown me repeatedly that it is contrary to the Bible to make any provision for our temporal wants in the time of trouble. I saw that if the saints had food laid up by them or in the field in the time of trouble, when sword, famine, and pestilence are in the land, it would be taken from them by violent hands and strangers would reap the fields. Then will be the time for us to trust wholly in God, and He will sustain us. I saw that our bread and water would be sure at that time, and we should not lack, or suffer hunger. The Lord has shown me that some of His children would fear when they see the price of food rising, and they would buy food and lay it by for the time of trouble. Then in a time of need, I saw them go to their food and look at it, and it had bred worms, and was full of living creatures, and not fit for use."*

Concerning the question of starvation, *Testimonies*, Vol. 1, p. 206 states: *"The time of trouble is just before us; and then stern necessity will require the people of God to deny self, and to eat merely enough to sustain life; but God will prepare us for that time. In that fearful hour our necessity will be God's opportunity to impart His strengthening power, and to sustain His people."* God wants to give us that blessing.

Early Writings, p. 56, further addresses the question of starvation. *"I saw that our bread and water will be sure at that time, and that we shall not lack or suffer hunger; for God is able to spread a table for us in the wilderness. If necessary He would send ravens to feed us, as He did to feed Elijah, or rain manna from heaven, as He did for the Israelites."* Praise the Lord!

During the Time of Jacob's Trouble, Satan and his evil angels are extremely active. In *The Great Controversy*, p. 635, the servant of the Lord describes it this way. *"The people of God—some in prison cells, some hidden in solitary retreats in the forests and the mountains—still plead for divine protection, while in every quarter companies of armed men, urged on by hosts of evil angels, are preparing for the work of death."* The evil angels will be very active in encouraging the world to put to death those who honor God and His Ten Commandments and honor Jesus as their Creator by keeping God's Sabbath holy.

The Time of Jacob's Trouble is further described in *Spiritual Gifts*, Vol. 3, pp. 132, 133. *"Jacob took firm hold of the angel in his distress, and would not let him go. As he made supplication with tears, the angel reminded him of his past wrongs, and endeavored to escape from Jacob, to test him and prove him. So will the righteous, in the day of their anguish, be tested, proved, and tried, to manifest their strength of faith, their perseverance and unshaken confidence in the power of God to deliver them."* God's people will be tested in a mighty way during this time period.

Why, then, does this test come upon God's true people who have already been judged to be saved? The answer to this question is given to us in *The Great Controversy*, pp. 618, 619. *"As Satan influenced Esau to march against Jacob, so he will stir up the wicked to destroy God's people in the time of trouble. And as he accused Jacob, he will urge his accusations against the people of God. He numbers the world as his subjects; but the little company who keep the commandments of God are resisting his supremacy. If he could blot them from the earth, his triumph would be complete. He sees that holy angels are guarding them, and he infers that their sins have been pardoned; but he does not know that their cases have been decided in the sanctuary above. He has an accurate knowledge of the sins which he has tempted them to commit, and he presents these before God in the most exaggerated light, representing this people to be just as deserving as himself of exclusion from the favor of God. He declares that the Lord cannot in justice forgive their sins and yet destroy him and his angels. He claims them as his prey and demands that they be given into his hands to destroy.*

As Satan accuses the people of God on account of their sins, the Lord permits him to try them to the uttermost. Their confidence in God, their faith and firmness, will be severely tested. As they review the past their hopes sink; for in their whole lives they can see little good. They are fully conscious of their weakness and unworthiness. Satan endeavors to terrify them with the thought that their cases are hopeless, that the stain of their defilement will never be washed away. He hopes so to destroy their faith that they will yield to his temptations and turn from their allegiance to God." Apparently, the accusations of Satan are the cause of the test during the Time of Jacob's Trouble. In fact, it is Satan that does the testing, as he tries to terrify us with the thought that our cases are hopeless. The righteous respond by wrestling with God day and night for assurance of pardon and deliverance from the wicked that surround them.

Other Reasons

Obviously, the main reason God's people are tested is due to Satan's accusations. However, it appears to me that there are other reasons.

In *The Great Controversy*, p. 621, is the following statement. *"The assaults of Satan are fierce and determined, his delusions are terrible; but the Lord's eye is upon His people, and His ear listens to their cries. Their affliction is great, the flames of the furnace seem about to consume them; but the Refiner will bring them forth as gold tried in the fire. God's love for His children during the period of their severest trial is as strong and tender as in the days of their sunniest prosperity, but it is needful for them to be placed in the furnace of fire; their earthliness must be consumed, that the image of Christ may be perfectly reflected."* We learned earlier that prior to the Close of Probation as a Point in Time; everyone who is saved has become a holy person and received the Seal of God. Now, during the Great Time of Trouble, we are told that we must go through the furnace of fire to consume the earthliness we still have. Apparently, even though we are holy and can follow all of God's Ten Commandments, there is still some earthliness that must be consumed "that the image of Christ may be perfectly reflected." This is another reason for the test during the Time of Jacob's Trouble.

In addition, while God knows who are saved and can be trusted in heaven, the angels of heaven and residents of the unfallen worlds do not know who can be trusted in heaven (unless they were present during every minute of the judgment). In fact, Satan, due to his accusations, has probably created some doubt. As they watch God's true people being tested during the Time of Jacob's Trouble, see them stand for Jesus even in the face of death, due to their faith; see them wrestle with God in fervent prayer to be assured of the pardon of their sins, and see the anguish that those who are saved go through, the angels of heaven and residents of the unfallen worlds will see that these people sincerely love Jesus and can be trusted in heaven. A voice from the throne then says "it is done," as God's people triumphantly come through the Time of Jacob's Trouble and are now ready for the Second Coming of Christ.

During the Time of Jacob's Trouble we must have come to the point where we are able to fully trust in God and be as faithful as Job was in saying, *"Though he slay me, yet will I trust in him"* (Job 13:15).

Also, the test must come to those who profess to be God's people in order to reveal the tares that still remain in God's church. The tares will not be able to stand during this final test.

In *The Great Controversy*, pp. 619, 620, are the following statements. *"Though God's people will be surrounded by enemies who are bent upon their destruction, yet the anguish which they suffer is not a dread of persecution for the truth's sake; they fear that every sin has not been repented of, and that through some fault in themselves they will fail to realize the fulfillment of the Saviour's promise: I 'will keep thee from the hour of temptation, which shall come upon all the world.' Revelation 3:10. If they could have the assurance of pardon, they would not shrink from torture or death; but should they prove unworthy, and lose their lives because of their own defects of character, then God's holy name would be reproached."* You see, at this time, God's true people, because of their love for Jesus Christ, are concerned not so much with the persecution, but with their pardon and the fear that if they don't prove worthy, God's holy name will be reproached.

Continuing further on: *"They afflict their souls before God, pointing to their past repentance of their many sins, and pleading the Saviour's promise: 'Let him take hold of My strength, that he may make peace with Me; and he shall make peace with Me.' Isaiah 27:5. Their faith does not fail because their prayers are not immediately answered. Though suffering the keenest anxiety, terror, and distress, they do not cease their intercessions. They lay hold of the strength of God as Jacob laid hold of the Angel; and the language of their souls is: 'I will not let Thee go, except Thou bless me.'"* The saints hold on to Jesus for dear life!

What follows next is described in *The Great Controversy*, pp. 632, 633. *"As the wrestling ones urge their petitions before God, the veil separating them from the unseen seems almost withdrawn. The heavens glow with the dawning of eternal day, and like the melody of angel songs, the words fall upon the ear, 'Stand fast to your allegiance. Help is coming.' . . . The precious Saviour will send help just when we need it."* Amen.

The Fourth, Fifth, and Sixth Plagues

Let's continue with the description of the plagues in Revelation 16:8-12. *"And the fourth angel poured out his vial upon the sun; and power was given unto him to scorch men with fire. And men were scorched with great heat, and blasphemed the name of God, which hath power over these plagues: and they repented not to give him glory."* Why don't the people repent? The Holy Spirit has been withdrawn from those that are lost! The Spirit is no longer leading them toward repentance! They therefore will not repent.

In this fourth plague the earth is scorched with the sun. Why? Apostate Christianity worships on the sun's day! The Lord is making a statement, if you want the sun, I'll give you the sun.

This fourth plague, which is again regional, has great heat, and causes a major famine, since plants cannot grow under the scorching heat of the sun.

"And the fifth angel poured out his vial upon the seat of the beast; and his kingdom was full of darkness; and they gnawed their tongues for pain, And blasphemed the God of heaven because of their pains and their sores, and repented not of their deeds." This fifth plague is poured out on the seat of the beast, the Roman Catholic Papacy. The kingdom is full of darkness. Why does the Roman Catholic Papacy receive the plague of darkness? They have deceived much of the Christian world and led millions of Christians into spiritual darkness. They therefore receive the plague of darkness. What do you think will be said, then, by those who follow the Roman Catholic Papacy and Apostate Protestantism in worshipping on the Venerable Day of the Sun? They would be questioning whether they are on the correct side of the Sabbath/Sunday question wouldn't they?

"And the sixth angel poured out his vial upon the great river Euphrates; and the water thereof was dried up, that the way of the kings of the east might be prepared." This sixth plague, most scholars believe, is symbolic. Who is Babylon? Of course, Babylon is called a whore in Revelation 17, and represents the false churches. What does the river Euphrates represent? Well, the Euphrates River flowed through the center of Babylon. It was the city's lifeline. It was Babylon's supply of water. What is water in symbolic Bible prophecy? It is multitudes of people from diverse backgrounds and cultures (Rev. 17:15). Babylon, the false churches, is supported by the Euphrates River, which represents multitudes of people. However, in Revelation 16 we find that the Euphrates, the multitudes of people that supported Babylon, the false churches, is dried up. Why? Due to the fact the multitudes of people have seen the fifth plague poured out on the seat of the beast, the Roman Catholic Papacy. They wonder if they are on the correct side of the Sabbath/Sunday question, and begin to withdraw their support. This delays the Whore Babylon's and Satan's quest, which is to kill all of God's true people.

The Bible says that this is done *"that the way of the kings of the east might be prepared."* Who are the kings of the east? Revelation 7:2 gives us some insight into this question. *"And I saw another angel ascending from the east".* You see, heaven's angels, and the Lord, always ascend or descend from the east or the north in Bible prophecy. Satan and his evil angels ascend or descend from the west or the south. That these kings come from the east indicates that they are from heaven. And who are the kings of heaven? They are, of course, God the Father, God the Son, and God the Holy Spirit. This prophecy reveals that the way for the kings of the east, along with all of heaven's angels, to come at the Second Coming of Christ is being prepared. Jesus is about to return at this time!

Verses 13 and 14 state, *"And I saw three unclean spirits like frogs come out of the mouth of the dragon, and out of the mouth of the beast, and out of the mouth of the false prophet. For they are the spirits of devils, working miracles, which go forth unto the kings of the earth and of the whole world, to gather them to the battle of that great day of God Almighty."* What is this battle of that great day of God Almighty? The Battle of Armageddon, of course! Three unclean spirits (evil angels) like frogs come out of the mouth of the dragon, who is Satan, the Beast, the Roman Catholic Papacy, and the False Prophet, Apostate Protestantism. The Bible says they are the spirits of devils working miracles, which is a reference to evil angels impersonating our dead loved ones. Remember, the fifth plague has been poured out on the Roman Catholic Papacy, and as a result, support is withdrawn from the Papacy and Apostate Protestantism. To counteract this withdrawal of support, Satan and his evil angels impersonate their dead loved ones to deceive the lost, get them to return to Satan's side of the Sabbath/Sunday question and continue on in their quest to kill all of God's true people. The lost will respond to this deception and are gathered together for the Battle of Armageddon.

The Spirit of Prophecy comments on this deception in *The Great Controversy*, pp. 561, 562. *"Satan has long been preparing for his final effort to deceive the world. The foundation of his work was laid by the assurance given to Eve in Eden: 'Ye shall not surely die.' 'In the day ye eat thereof, then your eyes shall be opened, and ye shall be as gods, knowing good and evil.' Genesis 3:4, 5. Little by little he has prepared the way for his masterpiece of deception in the development of spiritualism. He has not yet reached the full accomplishment of his designs; but it will be reached in the last remnant of time. Says the prophet: 'I saw three unclean spirits like frogs; ...they are the spirits of devils, working miracles, which go forth unto the kings of the earth and of the whole world, to gather them to the battle of that great day of God*

Almighty.' Revelation 16:13, 14. Except those who are kept by the power of God, through faith in His word, the whole world will be swept into the ranks of this delusion."

In Revelation 16:15, 16 Jesus says, *"Behold, I come as a thief. Blessed is he that watcheth, and keepeth his garments, lest he walk naked, and they see his shame. And he gathered them together into a place called in the Hebrew tongue Armageddon."* What are our garments? The righteousness of Jesus Christ that we must be putting on now! Through our relationship with Jesus we allow Him to put on those garments to prepare us for His Second Coming. However, Satan will do everything in his power to take those garments from us. At this time period everyone on planet earth is gathered together into a place called in the Hebrew tongue, Armageddon.

Ellen G. White encourages us with this statement in the *Review and Herald*, Aug.12, 1884. *"Let none be discouraged in view of the severe trials to be met in the time of Jacob's trouble, which is yet before them. They are to work earnestly, anxiously, not for that time, but for today. What we want is to have knowledge of the truth as it is in Christ now, and a personal experience now. In these precious closing hours of probation, we have a deep and living experience to gain. We shall thus form characters that will insure our deliverance in the time of trouble."* The time is now, friend, to spend that time with Jesus on a daily basis and allow Him to prepare you for the Time of Trouble and for His Second Coming.

Chapter 6

The Battle of Armageddon, the Seventh Plague, & the Second Coming of Christ

As those who are lost seek to kill and destroy those who are saved, we come to a time period the Bible calls *Armageddon*. Ellen White makes a comforting statement concerning this time period in *Early Writings*, p. 284. *"I saw that the people of God, who had faithfully warned the world of His coming wrath, would be delivered. God would not suffer the wicked to destroy those who were expecting translation and who would not bow to the decree of the beast or receive his mark. I saw that if the wicked were permitted to slay the saints, Satan and all his evil host, and all who hate God, would be gratified. And oh, what a triumph it would be for his satanic majesty to have power, in the last closing struggle, over those who had so long waited to behold Him whom they loved."* Satan and his evil angels will not have the power to kill one of God's true people. No one who is on the Lord's side will lose his or her life during the Great Time of Trouble. What a blessing that will be! Only during the Little Time of Trouble will there be some martyrs amongst God's true people, as we previously discovered.

We have seen the statement in Revelation 16:16, *"And he gathered them together into a place called in the Hebrew tongue Armageddon."* The world believes that this war called the Battle of Armageddon will be fought in Israel in what is called the Valley of Megiddo. They take

Revelation 16:12 literally rather than symbolically, and insist that the kings of the east are the Chinese. The Chinese cross the river Euphrates when it dries up and they enter the Valley of Megiddo to fight the Battle of Armageddon, with all of the world's population gathered there. This belief is so ridiculous it does not even bear consideration! First of all, why do the Chinese need the river Euphrates to dry up to cross it? With modern-day planes and helicopters, the drying up of the river Euphrates is not necessary to cross it!

Second, all of the world's population would need to arrive at the Valley of Megiddo. It is estimated that the Valley of Megiddo could hold five million people at most, less than the total population of New York City and the population of many other cities of the world. How, then, could the Valley of Megiddo contain seven billion people, the world's population? This is literally impossible!

Third, Leo Schreven, of *It Is Written* television, a fellow evangelist, states that he did a study to determine how long it would take to fly the entire world's population to the Valley of Megiddo utilizing the current flight schedules. His estimate was one hundred and sixty years! The idea that the Battle of Armageddon will be fought in the Valley of Megiddo is completely absurd! Revelation 16:12 should be taken symbolically.

What, then, is the Battle of Armageddon, and where will it be fought? The Bible says the world will be gathered to a place called in the Hebrew tongue *Armageddon*. While there is no place in the Hebrew language with the name Armageddon, many Biblical experts believe that the term comes from two Hebrew words *Har* and *Megiddon* (see *Strong's Concordance*). The Hebrew word Har means "mountain." The Hebrew word Megiddon comes from the Hebrew term Megiddow and means "Megiddo." Therefore, *Armageddon* in the Hebrew tongue means "mountain Megiddo." Notice that it does not mean "Valley of Megiddo." Its meaning is *mountain Megiddo*. What does *Megiddow* mean? It means "rendezvous," and comes from the root word gadad which means "to assemble or gather." As we put these terms together we come to the conclusion that the term *Armageddon* in the Hebrew tongue means "mountain rendezvous, assembly or gathering." Since there is no particular mountain on planet earth that could hold a gathering of seven billion people, the term must have symbolic meaning.

What is a mountain in symbolic Bible prophecy? Well, in Revelation 17 we find a whore sitting on seven mountains with seven kings. The mountain is symbolic of a world kingdom. Jeremiah 51:24, 25 confirms this fact as it describes Babylon, a world kingdom, as being a mountain. *"And I will render unto Babylon and to all the inhabitants of Chaldea all their evil that they have done in Zion in your sight, saith the LORD. Behold, I am against thee, O destroying mountain, saith the LORD, which destroyest all the earth: and I will stretch out mine hand upon thee, and roll thee down from the rocks, and will make thee a burnt mountain."*

Also, in Daniel 2, God's kingdom, a world kingdom of course, was to be set up after all the nations, symbolized by metals in the image King Nebuchadnezzar dreamt about, are destroyed. In the description of this dream, Daniel 2:34, 35 describes God's world kingdom as a mountain. *"Thou sawest till that a stone was cut out without hands, which smote the image upon his feet that were of iron and clay, and brake them to pieces. Then was the iron, the clay, the brass, the silver, and the gold, broken to pieces together, and became like the chaff of the summer threshingfloors; and the wind carried them away, that no place was found for them: and the stone that smote the image became a great mountain, and filled the whole earth."* An explanation of the mountain is given in verse 44. *"And in the days of these kings shall the God of heaven set up a kingdom, which shall never be destroyed: and the kingdom shall not be left to other people, but it shall break in pieces and consume all these kingdoms, and it shall stand for ever."* Mountains in symbolic Bible prophecy are world kingdoms.

In conclusion, then, the term Armageddon in the Hebrew tongue refers to a world kingdom rendezvous, assembly, or gathering. This is exactly what the Battle of Armageddon is; a worldwide gathering of a world kingdom comprised of Satan, his evil angels, and his people, those who are lost; against a world kingdom comprised of Jesus, His angels, and God's people, those who are saved. These are spiritual world kingdoms, not physical, and therefore both can exist worldwide at the same time.

This battle is described in *Early Writings*, pp. 283, 284, as God's people worldwide are worried because the wicked are preparing to kill them. *"Soon I saw the saints suffering great mental anguish. They seemed to be surrounded by the wicked inhabitants of the earth. Every appearance was against them. Some began to fear that God had at last left them to perish by the hand of the wicked. But if their eyes could have been opened, they would have seen themselves surrounded by angels of God. Next came the multitude of the angry wicked, and next a mass of evil angels, hurrying on the wicked to slay the saints. But before they could approach God's people, the wicked must first pass this company of mighty, holy angels. This was impossible. The angels of God were causing them to recede and also causing the evil angels who were pressing around them to fall back."* Amen. Praise the Lord! God's angels are our defense!

"It was an hour of fearful, terrible agony to the saints. Day and night they cried unto God for deliverance. To outward appearance, there was no possibility of their escape. The wicked had already begun to triumph, crying out, "Why doesn't your God deliver you out of our hands? Why don't you go up and save your lives?" But the saints heeded them not, Like Jacob, they were wrestling with God." What a time this will be for God's people!

The Battle of Armageddon is summarized in Revelation 17:12-14. *"And the ten horns which thou sawest are ten kings, which have received no kingdom as yet; but receive power as kings one hour with the beast. These have one mind, and shall give their power and strength unto the beast. These shall make war with the Lamb, and the Lamb shall overcome them: for he is Lord of lords, and King of kings: and they that are with him are called, and chosen, and faithful."* This text describes the merging of the Beast power, or False Christianity, and the kingdoms of this world, for a very short time—a merger of church and state. This is the final phase of the Whore Babylon power described in Revelation 17, in which Apostate Protestantism combines with Papal Rome, and the two combine with the governments of this world, (For a full explanation of the purpose and meaning of the Whore Babylon with its seven heads, please see my book entitled *The Final Catastrophic Events*). What is the purpose of this merger? To make war with the Lamb, Jesus Christ, and the people who are with Him, God's true people, His saints. These texts describe the Battle of Armageddon; a war between Satan, his angels, and his people led by the Antichrist, and Jesus, His angels, and His people.

In this battle Satan, his angels, and his people surround God's people, who are protected by heaven's angels. Revelation 16:17, 18 describes what happens next. *"And the seventh angel poured out his vial into the air; and there came a great voice out of the temple of heaven, from the throne, saying, It is done. And there were voices, and thunders, and lightnings; and there was a great earthquake, such as was not since men were upon the earth, so mighty an earthquake, and so great."* As Satan's people surround the saints, ready to destroy God's true people, suddenly a voice is heard from heaven as the seventh plague is poured out upon earth, amidst voices and thunders and lightnings. This first phase of the seventh plague is an earthquake, the worst earthquake ever to occur on planet earth.

This time period, which includes a very special additional event, is described in *Early Writings,* p. 285. *"It was at midnight that God chose to deliver His people. As the wicked were mocking around them, suddenly the sun appeared, shining in his strength, and the moon stood still. The wicked looked upon the scene with amazement, while the saints beheld with solemn joy the tokens of their deliverance. Signs and wonders followed in quick succession. Everything seemed turned out of its natural course. The streams ceased to flow. Dark, heavy clouds came up and clashed against each other. But there was one clear place of settled glory, whence came the voice of God like many waters, shaking the heavens and the earth. There was a mighty earthquake. The graves were opened, and those who had died in faith under the third angel's message, keeping the Sabbath, came forth from their dusty beds, glorified, to hear the covenant of peace that God was to make with those who had kept His law."* This passage describes a Special Resurrection that will occur at this time.

This Special Resurrection is further described in *The Great Controversy,* p. 637. *"Graves are opened, and 'many of them that sleep in the dust of the earth. . . . awake, some to everlasting life, and some to shame and everlasting contempt. Daniel 12:2. All who have died in the faith of the third angel's message come forth from the tomb glorified, to hear God's covenant of peace with those who have kept His law. 'They also which pierced Him' (Revelation 1:7), those that mocked and derided Christ's dying agonies, and the most violent opposers of His truth and His people, are raised to behold Him in His glory, and to see the honor placed upon the loyal and obedient."* What irony! Those that have persecuted Jesus and His people to the largest extent, believing they were correct, will be raised from the dead to behold Jesus in His glory and see the honor placed on the people whom they despised and persecuted!

The earthquake, the voice from heaven, and the Special Resurrection occur, and *Testimonies for the Church*, Vol. 1, p. 354, describes what happens next. *"The captivity of the righteous is turned, and with sweet and solemn whisperings they say to one another: "We are delivered. It is the voice of God." With solemn awe they listen to the words of the voice. The wicked hear, but understand not the words of the voice of God. They fear and tremble, while the saints rejoice."* Notice that at this time the wicked cannot understand the Voice of God. However, we will discover that a short time later the tables are turned and the opposite occurs, the wicked will understand what is being said to them by God while at that time the righteous will not understand.

What is said by God at this time is revealed in *The Great Controversy*, p. 640. *"The voice of God is heard from heaven, declaring the day and hour of Jesus' coming, and delivering the everlasting covenant to His people. Like peals of loudest thunder, His words roll through the earth."*

Early Writings, p. 15, states, *"The living saints, 144,000 in number, knew and understood the voice, while the wicked thought it was thunder and an earthquake. When God spoke the time, He poured upon us the Holy Ghost, and our faces began to light up and shine with the glory of God, as Moses' did when he came down from Mount Sinai."* Remember previously, as we examined the texts concerning the 144,000, we found that there is an initial group called the 144,000 who give the Loud Cry to the rest of the world, and millions join the 144,000 to stand for God in the final stages of this world's history. And then, as indicated in the above passage, in the Great Time of Trouble this group is still called the 144,000. This leads us to believe that the number 144,000 is symbolic of God's true church, His saints, symbolized in Revelation 7 as 12,000 per tribe of the twelve tribes of Israel, which do not physically exist, and must be symbolic. Ellen White sees 144,000 in order to identify the entity, God's perfected church, His true people.

These 144,000, symbolic of all of God's true people, are able to understand the Voice of God at this time in history but the wicked think it is thunder and an earthquake.

Continuing in *Early Writings*, p. 15, *"The 144,000 were all sealed and perfectly united. On their foreheads was written, God, New Jerusalem, and a glorious star containing Jesus' new name. At our happy, holy state the wicked were enraged, and would rush violently up to lay hands on us to thrust us into prison, when we would stretch forth the hand in the name of the Lord, and they would fall helpless to the ground. Then it was that the synagogue of Satan knew that God had loved us who could wash one another's feet and salute the brethren with a holy kiss, and they worshiped at our feet."* Where this occurs, the tables are turned, and the wicked on the front lines now realize they are on the wrong side of the Sabbath/Sunday conflict.

The Voice of God is further described in *Early Writings*, p. 34. *"God spoke the day and the hour of Jesus' coming and delivered the everlasting covenant to His people, He spoke one sentence, and then paused, while the words were rolling through the earth. The Israel of God stood with their eyes fixed upward, listening to the words as they came from the mouth of Jehovah, and rolled through the earth like peals of loudest thunder. It was awfully solemn. And at the end of every sentence the saints shouted, "Glory, Alleluia!" Their countenances were lighted up with the glory of God; and they shone with the glory, as did the face of Moses when he came down from Sinai. The wicked could not look on them for the glory. And when the never-ending blessing was pronounced on those who had honored God in keeping His Sabbath holy, there was a mighty shout of victory over the beast and over his image."*

At this time the countenance of those who are saved greatly differs from the countenance of those that are lost as described in *Early Writings*, pp. 272, 273. *"A glorious light shone upon them. How beautiful they then looked! All marks of care and weariness were gone, and health and beauty were seen in every countenance. Their enemies, the heathen around them, fell like dead men; they could not endure the light that shone upon the delivered, holy ones. This light and glory remained upon them, until Jesus was seen in the clouds of heaven . . ."*

This time period of the Voice of God, which is not understood by the wicked, is further described in *The Great Controversy*, pp. 635, 636. *"With shouts of triumph, jeering, and imprecation, throngs of evil men are about to rush upon their prey, when, lo, a dense blackness, deeper than the darkness of the night, falls upon the earth. Then a rainbow, shining with the glory from the throne of God, spans the heavens and seems to encircle each praying company. The angry multitudes are suddenly arrested. Their mocking cries die away. The objects of their murderous rage are forgotten. With fearful forebodings they gaze upon the symbol of God's covenant and long to be shielded from its overpowering brightness.*

By the people of God a voice, clear and melodious, is heard, saying, "Look up," and lifting their eyes to the heavens, they behold the bow of promise. The black, angry clouds that covered the firmament are parted, and like Stephen they look up steadfastly into heaven and see the glory of God and the Son of man seated upon His throne. In His divine form they discern the marks of His humiliation; and from His lips they hear the request presented before His Father and the holy angels: 'I will that they also, whom Thou hast given Me, be with Me where I am.' John 17:24. Again a voice, musical and triumphant, is heard, saying: 'They come! They come; holy, harmless, and undefiled. They have kept the word of My patience; they shall walk among the angels;" and the pale, quivering lips of those who have held fast their faith utter a shout of victory.

It is at midnight that God manifests His power for the deliverance of His people. The sun appears, shining in its strength. Signs and wonders follow in quick succession. The wicked look with terror and amazement upon the scene, while the righteous behold with solemn joy the tokens of their deliverance. Everything in nature seems turned out of its course. The streams cease to flow. Dark, heavy clouds come up and clash against each other. In the midst of the angry heavens is one clear space of indescribable glory, whence comes the voice of God like the sound of many waters, saying: 'It is done.' Revelation 16:17." At this point, it is finished; God's people have passed the final test during the Time of Jacob's Trouble, and as revealed earlier, all of heaven's angels and those from unfallen worlds now know that these individuals are worthy to be in the kingdom of heaven.

The Great Controversy, pp. 637, 638 states, *"Thick clouds still cover the sky; yet the sun now and then breaks through, appearing like the avenging eye of Jehovah. Fierce lightnings leap from the heavens, enveloping the earth in a sheet of flame. Above the terrific roar of thunder, voices, mysterious and awful, declare the doom of the wicked. The words spoken are not comprehended by all; but they are distinctly understood by the false teachers. Those who a little before were so reckless, so boastful and defiant, so exultant in their cruelty to God's commandment-keeping people, are now overwhelmed with consternation and shuddering in fear. Their wails are heard above the sound of the elements. Demons acknowledge the deity of Christ and tremble before His power, while men are supplicating for mercy and groveling in abject terror."* At this juncture the wicked, especially the false teachers, understand the Voice of God, but what a time this will be for those who would not follow Jesus and all of His Ten Commandments.

The Great Controversy, pp. 639, 640 states, *"Then there appears against the sky a hand holding two tables of stone folded together. . . . The hand opens the tables, and there are seen the precepts of the Decalogue, traced as with a pen of fire."* These tables of stone are opened and the wicked see the Ten Commandments. Even if they have not been on the front lines every person on planet earth among the wicked now realize that they definitely are on the wrong side and have been deceived.

"The words are so plain that all can read them. Memory is aroused, the darkness of superstition and heresy is swept from every mind, and God's ten words, brief, comprehensive, and authoritative are presented to the view of all the inhabitants of the earth.

It is impossible to describe the horror and despair of those who have trampled upon God's holy requirements. The Lord gave them His law; they might have compared their characters with it and learned their defects while there was yet opportunity for repentance and reform; but in order to secure the favor of the world, they set aside its precepts and taught others to transgress. They have endeavored to compel God's people to profane His Sabbath. Now they are condemned by that law which they have despised. With awful distinctness they see that they are without excuse. . . . The enemies of God's law, from the ministers down to the least among them, have a new conception of truth and duty. Too late they see that the Sabbath of the fourth com-mandment is the seal of the living God. Too late they see the true nature of their spurious sabbath and the sandy foundation upon which they have been building. They find that they have been fighting against God." Can you imagine coming to the end of your life and finding out all along you were fighting against God! This will be the experience of many people as we approach the end of this world!

Now that they realize they are lost and have been deceived by their religious leaders, what do the people and the leaders of this world do next? Revelation 17:16 reveals the answer to this question. *"And the ten horns which thou sawest upon the beast, these shall hate the whore, and shall make her desolate and naked, and shall eat her flesh, and burn her with fire."* You see, the leaders of this world now understand they have been deceived by the false churches, symbolized as the Whore Babylon, and therefore turn against the religious powers that deceived them, to destroy them. All of those religious leaders, those Sunday-keeping pastors, those people who have professed to follow Jesus Christ but have led others into the observance of the Venerable Day of the Sun are turned against by the rest of the world. This will be a very awful time for those who have misled the people on earth and caused the loss of their salvation.

In addition, as many people who claimed to be followers of God re-alize they were also deceived by evil spirits impersonating their dead loved ones, they will react in a way described in *This Day with God*, p. 312, as follows: *"When these spiritualistic deceptions are revealed to be what they really are—the secret workings of evil spirits—those who have acted a part in them will become as men who have lost their minds."* As these people realize they have been deceived by evil angels, they literally lose their minds and, one can assume, will turn on the re-ligious leaders who also deceived them, with a vengeance. This will be an awful time for those Sunday-keeping pastors who refuse to follow Jesus and all of His Ten Commandments.

Revelation 16:18-21 describes what occurs during this time period when the Voice of God is heard along with thunders and lightnings and the Ten Commandments are revealed in the sky. *"And there were voices, and thunders, and lightnings; and there was a great earth-quake, such as was not since men were upon the earth, so mighty an earthquake, and so great. And the great city was divided into three parts, and the cities of the nations fell: and great Babylon came in remembrance before God, to give unto her the cup of the wine of the fierceness of his wrath. And every island fled away, and the mountains were not found. And there fell upon men a great hail out of heaven, every stone about the weight of a talent: and men blasphemed God because of the plague of the hail; for the plague thereof was exceeding great."*

The Spirit of Prophecy further describes this time period in *The Great Controversy*, pp. 636, 637, as follows: *"That voice shakes the heavens and the earth. There is a mighty earthquake, 'such as was not since men were upon the earth, so mighty an earthquake, and so great.' Verses 17, 18. The firmament appears to open and shut. The glory from the throne of God seems flashing through. The mountains shake like a reed in the wind, and ragged rocks are scattered on every side. There is a roar as of a coming tempest. The sea is lashed into fury. There is heard the shriek of a hurricane like the voice of demons upon a mission of destruction. The whole earth heaves and swells like the waves of the sea. Its surface is breaking up. Its very foundations seem to be giving way. Mountain chains are sinking. Inhabited islands disappear. The seaports that have become like Sodom for wickedness are swallowed up by the angry waters. Babylon the great has come in remembrance before God, "to give unto her the cup of the wine of the fierceness of His wrath." Great hailstones, every one "about the weight of a talent," are doing their work of destruction."*

What is the weight of a talent? There are various estimates, but most Bibles give this weight as between eighty and one hundred and fifty pounds. These hailstones are huge, and wreak unbelievable havoc upon planet earth. It is well known that a penny dropped from the Empire State Building could split the skull and kill an individual on the ground. Imagine the damage that will be caused by this plague, with hailstones that come from miles above and weigh as much as one hundred and fifty pounds. In addition, a great earthquake will occur, the magnitude of which has never been seen here on planet earth. Islands will be under the sea and mountains will crumble and disappear from the force of this great earthquake. This earth will be reduced to utter ruin.

You'll also notice that those who survive this plague blaspheme God. The Holy Spirit has been withdrawn and they continue throughout the Seven Last Plagues to blaspheme God. They will not change their mind or heart. The judgment has already passed.

As this seventh plague hits planet earth, Jesus begins His return. The heavens departing as a scroll is described in *Early Writings*, p. 41. *"Dark, heavy clouds came up and clashed against each other. The atmosphere parted and rolled back; then we could look up through the open space in Orion, whence came the voice of God."*

As Jesus begins His return, the reaction of those who survive the seventh plague and are lost is found in Revelation 6:14-17. *"And the heaven departed as a scroll when it is rolled together; and every mountain and island were moved out of their places. And the kings of the earth, and the great men, and the rich men, and the chief captains, and the mighty men, and every bondman, and every free man, hid themselves in the dens and in the rocks of the mountains; And said to the mountains and rocks, Fall on us, and hide us from the face of him that sitteth on the throne, and from the wrath of the Lamb: For the great day of his wrath is come; and who shall be able to stand?"* Those who are saved have come out of the dens and rocks from whence they were hiding to hear the Voice of God, see the Ten Commandments written in the sky, and meet their Lord in the air at His Second Coming. Those who are lost now take the place of those who are saved in the dens and rocks of the mountains. Why? They cannot, with their frail, sinful human bodies, stand in the sight of our living God and millions and millions of angels as they descend toward this earth. Remember, the wicked fell down like dead men when the brightness of the glory of our Lord shone upon those who are saved. The brightness of Jesus and the Father and millions of angels cannot be withstood by the human body. They therefore seek the darkness of the caves and dens and rocks to escape the brightness of the glory of the Second Coming of Jesus Christ.

Maranatha, p. 290, describes the experience of the lost as they enter the caves and dens. *"The people who have braved out their rebellion will fulfill the description given in Revelation 6:15-17. In these very caves and dens [where God's people have been hiding] they find the very statement of truth in the letters and in the publications as witness against them. The shepherds who lead the sheep in false paths will hear the charge made against them, 'It was you who made light of truth. It was you who told us that God's law was abrogated, that it was a yoke of bondage. It was you who voiced the false doctrines when I was convicted that these Seventh-day Adventists had the truth. The blood of our souls is upon your priestly garments.'* " Imagine their consternation when they realize they could have been on God's side of the Sabbath question and been saved, had they yielded to the working of the Holy Spirit instead of listening to their religious leaders. What an awful time this will be for those who are lost.

A summary of the time period we have covered over the last several paragraphs is given in a description of the Battle of Armageddon in Revelation 19:11-21, as John sees Jesus, *"And I saw heaven opened, and behold a white horse; and he that sat upon him was called Faithful and True, and in righteousness he doth judge and make war. His eyes were as a flame of fire, and on his head were many crowns; and he had a name written, that no man knew, but he himself. And he was clothed with a vesture dipped in blood: and his name is called The Word of God. And the armies which were in heaven followed him upon white horses, clothed in fine linen, white and clean. And out of his mouth goeth a sharp sword, that with it he should smite the nations: and he shall rule them with a rod of iron: and he treadeth the winepress of the fierceness and wrath of Almighty God."* Who are the armies in heaven that follow Jesus? Heaven's angels of course! The Bible declares that Jesus treads the winepress of the fierceness and wrath of Almighty God. What is the wrath of God? The Seven Last Plagues (Revelation 15:1). As Jesus begins His return with His angels, the wrath of God is being poured out in the form of the seventh plague. The great earthquake occurs, and hailstones, each the weight of a talent, are being poured out upon the earth causing great devastation.

"And he hath on his vesture and on his thigh a name written, KING OF KINGS, AND LORD OF LORDS. And I saw an angel standing in the sun; and he cried with a loud voice, saying to all the fowls that fly in the midst of heaven, Come and gather yourselves together unto the supper of the great God; That ye may eat the flesh of kings, and the flesh of captains, and the flesh of mighty men, and the flesh of horses, and of them that sit on them, and the flesh of all men, both free and bond, both small and great. And I saw the beast, and the kings of the

earth, and their armies, gathered together to make war against him that sat on the horse, and against his army." When they gather against God's true people, they gather against God. Once the death decree is issued after the first plague and they then try to carry it out between the sixth and seventh plagues, Jesus responds with the Voice of God, the Ten Commandments in the sky, and the seventh plague as He begins His return with the Father and millions of angels.

"And the beast was taken, and with him the false prophet that wrought miracles before him, with which he deceived them that had received the mark of the beast, and them that worshipped his image. These both were cast alive into a lake of fire burning with brimstone. And the remnant were slain with the sword of him that sat upon the horse, which sword proceeded out of his mouth: and all the fowls were filled with their flesh." What is the sword by which the wicked are slain? *"And then shall that Wicked be revealed, whom the Lord shall consume with the spirit of his mouth, and shall destroy with the brightness of his coming"* (2 Thess. 2:8). The remnant of the wicked, those that are still alive after all of the plagues have completed their work, will be destroyed by the brightness of Jesus' coming. There will not be one person among the wicked that will be left alive. Jesus fights the Battle of Armageddon for His people. Amongst those who are saved, not one person will lose his or her life during the Great Time of Trouble! Praise the Lord!

The Second Coming is further described in *The Upward Look*, p. 261. *"In the day of His coming, the last great trumpet is heard, and there is a terrible shaking of earth and heaven. The whole earth, from the loftiest mountains to the deepest mines, will hear. Everything will be penetrated by fire. The tainted atmosphere will be cleansed by fire. The fire having fulfilled its mission, the dead that have been laid away in the grave will come forth—some to the resurrection of life, to be caught up to meet their Lord in the air, and some to behold the coming of Him whom they have despised and whom they now recognize as the Judge of all the earth.*

All the righteous are untouched by the flames. . . . Earthquakes, hurricanes, flame, and flood cannot injure those who are prepared to meet their Saviour in peace."

Manuscript Releases, Vol. 9, pp. 251, 252, describes this time period this way. *"Now in regard to the coming of the Son of man, This will not take place until after the mighty earthquake shakes the earth. After the people have heard the voice of God they are in despair and trouble such as never was since there was a nation, and in this the people of God will suffer affliction. The clouds of heaven will clash, and there will be darkness. Then that voice comes from heaven and the clouds begin to roll back like a scroll, and there is the bright, clear sign of the Son of Man. The children of God know what that cloud means.*

The sound of music is heard, and as it nears, the graves are opened and the dead are raised and there are thousands of thousands and ten thousand times ten thousand of angels that compose that glory, and encircle the Son of man. Those who have acted the most prominent part in the rejection and crucifixion of Christ come forth to see Him as he is, and those who have rejected Christ come up and see the saints glorified, and it is at that time that the saints are changed in a moment, in the twinkling of an eye, and are caught up to meet their Lord in the air." What a blessed day that will be! Families united, little children placed in their mother's arms, loved ones are united again!

Another description of the resurrection is given in *Spiritual Gifts*, Vol. 2, p. 33. *"Then Jesus' silver trumpet sounded, as he descended on the cloud, wrapped in flames of fire. He gazed on the graves of the sleeping saints, then raised his eyes and hands to heaven and cried, Awake! Awake! Awake! ye that sleep in the dust, and arise. Then there was a mighty earthquake. The graves opened, and the dead came up clothed with immortality. The 144,000 shouted, Hallelujah! as they recognized their friends who had been torn from them by death, and in the same moment we were changed and caught up together with them to meet the Lord in the air."*

Early Writings, pp. 287-289, describe with great detail the Second Coming of Christ as the voice of Jesus is heard to call forth from the grave all those sleeping in Christ. *"The earth mightily shook as the voice of the Son of God called forth the sleeping saints. They responded to the call and came forth clothed with glorious immortality, crying, 'Victory, victory, over death and the grave! O death, where is thy sting? O grave, where is thy victory?' Then the living saints and the risen ones raised their voices in a long, transporting shout of victory. Those bod-*

ies that had gone down into the grave bearing the marks of disease and death came up in immortal health and vigor. The living saints are changed in a moment, in the twinkling of an eye, and caught up with the risen ones, and together they meet their Lord in the air. Oh, what a glorious meeting! Friends whom death had separated were united, never more to part."

Early Writings, p. 16, states, *"We all entered the cloud together, and were seven days ascending to the sea of glass."* Seven days to get to heaven!

Continuing with *Early Writings*, pp. 287-289: *"On each side of the cloudy chariot were wings, and beneath it were living wheels; and as the chariot rolled upward, the wheels cried, "Holy," and the wings, as they moved, cried, "Holy," and the retinue of holy angels around the cloud cried, "Holy, holy, holy, Lord God Almighty!" And the saints in the cloud cried, "Glory! Alleluia!" And the chariot rolled upward to the Holy City. Before entering the city, the saints were arranged in a perfect square, with Jesus in the midst. He stood head and shoulders above the saints and above the angels. His majestic form and lovely countenance could be seen by all in the square.*

Then I saw a very great number of angels bring from the city glorious crowns—a crown for every saint, with his name written thereon. As Jesus called for the crowns, angels presented them to Him, and with His own right hand, the lovely Jesus placed the crowns on the heads of the saints. In the same manner the angels brought the harps, and Jesus presented them also to the saints. The commanding angels first struck the note, and then every voice was raised in grateful, happy praise, and every hand skillfully swept over the strings of the harp, sending forth melodious music in rich and perfect strains. Then I saw Jesus lead the redeemed company to the gate of the city. He laid hold of the gate and swung it back on its glittering hinges and bade the nations that had kept the truth enter in. Within the city there was everything to feast the eye. Rich glory they beheld everywhere. Then Jesus looked upon His redeemed saints; their countenances were radiant with glory; and as He fixed His loving eyes upon them, He said, with His rich, musical voice, "I behold the travail of My soul, and am satisfied. This rich glory is yours to enjoy eternally. Your sorrows are ended. There shall be no more death, neither sorrow nor crying, neither shall there be any more pain." I saw the redeemed host bow and cast their glittering crowns at the feet of Jesus, and then, as His lovely hand raised them up, they touched their golden harps and filled all heaven with their rich music and songs to the Lamb.

I then saw Jesus leading His people to the tree of life, and again we heard His lovely voice, richer than any music that ever fell on mortal ear, saying, "The leaves of this tree are for the healing of the nations. Eat ye all of it." Upon the tree of life was most beautiful fruit, of which the saints could partake freely. In the city was a most glorious throne, from which proceeded a pure river of water of life, clear as crystal. On each side of this river was the tree of life, and on the banks of the river were other beautiful trees bearing fruit which was good for food.

Language is altogether too feeble to attempt a description of heaven. As the scene rises before me, I am lost in amazement. Carried away with the surpassing splendor and excellent glory, I lay down the pen, and exclaim, "Oh, what love! What wondrous love!" The most exalted language fails to describe the glory of heaven or the matchless depths of a Saviour's love."

Summary

Early Writings, p. 110, describes the Second Coming of Christ, the condition of the saints, and the saints' response to Jesus at His Second Coming. *"All heaven will be emptied of the angels, while the waiting saints will be looking for Him and gazing into heaven, as were the men of Galilee when He ascended from the Mount of Olivet. Then only those who are holy, those who have followed fully the meek Pattern, will with rapturous joy exclaim as they behold Him, "Lo, this is our God; we have waited for Him, and He will save us." And they will be changed "in a moment, in the twinkling of an eye, at the last trump"*. I want to be there at that day to experience the Second Coming of Christ, don't you?

Throughout our study of these Final Events we have seen that the primary message communicated to us is to have a close relationship with Jesus; to spend the time with Him on a daily basis to allow Him to make us holy people. This will enable us to follow the Seventh-day

Sabbath and keep it holy, which is the pinnacle of the Ten Commandments, the Seal of God, and the main issue as we approach the end of this world. Once you have the ability to keep the Seventh-day Sabbath holy, because you have allowed Jesus to make you a holy person, you are now able to keep the other nine commandments holy as well.

We have also seen throughout this study that we have a lot of trying times ahead of us. Again, we must develop a strong relationship with Jesus and allow Him to prepare us for these Final Events, prepare us for heaven, and prepare us to stand for Him against all odds as we approach the end of this world.

The *Desire of Ages* summarizes this for us on page 324. *"The only defense against evil is the indwelling of Christ in the heart through faith in His righteousness. Unless we become vitally connected with God, we can never resist the unhallowed effects of self-love, self-indulgence, and temptation to sin. We may leave off many bad habits, for the time we may part company with Satan; but without a vital connection with God, through the surrender of ourselves to Him moment by moment, we shall be overcome. Without a personal acquaintance with Christ, and a continual communion, we are at the mercy of the enemy, and shall do his bidding in the end."*

I want to close this writing with good counsel from Jesus found in Matthew 24:13, *"But he that shall endure unto the end, the same shall be saved."* Whatever we must go through as we approach the end of this world, no matter how trying and hard it is, we must never, ever, ever give up. We must endure to the end.

Friend, spend the time with Jesus on a daily basis. Develop a strong love relationship with Him. This is the only part we have in preparation for these Final Events. Jesus will do all the rest. Jesus will make us holy people! Jesus will prepare us for His Second Coming! Jesus will prepare us for heaven! Jesus will give us the gift of eternal life! Amen.

---

[1] Marvin Moore, *The Crisis of the End Time*, pgs. 50-53
[2] G. Edward Reid, *Sunday's Coming*, pg. 77

[3] Ibid, pg. 76 from *American State Papers,* pg. 562

[4] Gaines M. Foster, article in *Church History*; Dec. 2002, Vol. 71 Issue 4, pg. 799, 21p

[5] Elson M. Haas, M.D., *Staying Healthy with Nutrition,* pg. 347

[6] Reported on 3ABN, January 6, 2006

[6] Leo Schreven, *Now That's Clear,* pg. 31

APPENDIX

Chapter 1

Duty in View of the Little Time of Trouble—Should we sell our homes?

This question is answered in *Early Writings, p. 57,* as follows: *"Houses and lands will be of no use to the saints in the time of trouble, for they will then have to flee before infuriated mobs, and at that time their possessions cannot be disposed of to advance the cause of present truth. I was shown that it is the will of God that the saints should cut loose from every encumbrance before the time of trouble comes, and make a covenant with God through sacrifice. If they have their property on the altar and earnestly inquire of God for duty, He will teach them when to dispose of these things. Then they will be free in the time of trouble and have no clogs to weigh them down.*

I saw that if any held on to their property and did not inquire of the Lord as to their duty, He would not make duty known, and they would be permitted to keep their property, and in the time of trouble it would come up before them like a mountain to crush them, and they would try to dispose of it, but would not be able. I heard some mourn like this: 'The cause was languishing, God's people were starving for the truth, and we made no effort to supply the lack; now our property is useless. Oh, that we had let it go, and laid up treasure in heaven!' I saw that a sacrifice did not increase, but it decreased and was consumed. I also saw that God had not required all of His people to dispose of their property at the same time; but if they desired to be taught, He would teach them, in a time of need, when to sell and how much to sell. Some have been required to dispose of their property in times past to sustain the Advent cause, while others have been permitted to keep theirs until a time of need. Then, as the cause needs it, their duty is to sell.

I saw that the message, 'Sell that ye have, and give alms,' has not been given, by some, in its clear light, and the object of the words of our Saviour has not been clearly presented. The object of selling is not to give to those who are able to labor and support themselves, but to spread the truth. It is a sin to support and indulge in idleness those who are able to labor. Some have been zealous to attend all the meetings, not to glorify God, but for the 'loaves and fishes.' Such would much better have been at home laboring with their hands, 'the thing that is good,' to supply the wants of their families and to have something to give to sustain the precious cause of present truth. Now is the time to lay up treasure in heaven and to set our hearts in order, ready for the time of trouble. Those only who have clean hands and pure hearts will stand in that trying time. Now is the time for the law of God to be in our minds, foreheads, and written in our hearts."

Chapter 2

Allowing the Bible and the Spirit of Prophecy to Interpret Itself—A Principle Violated by the Shepherd's Rod and Others

One of the key principles followed throughout this book has been that of allowing both the Bible and the Spirit of Prophecy writings to interpret themselves to obtain a correct understanding of the Final Events as we approach the end of this world. Unfortunately, there are many groups, such as the Shepherd's Rod, that have routinely violated this principle and interpreted the Spirit of Prophecy statements to suit themselves and the beliefs they want to embrace and promote throughout the Seventh-day Adventist Church.

During a camp meeting in New Jersey I was personally given some literature and CDs promoting some of the Shepherd's Rod beliefs, and found that while there were some good things expressed, intermingled with those good things were statements taken out of context from the Spirit of Prophecy writings to build a scenario that is false and misleading. A major example of this violation of the principle of allowing the Bible and the Spirit of Prophecy to interpret themselves follows.

One of the concepts promoted by the Shepherd's Rod is that the five agents of Ezekiel 9 that destroy the wicked in the church are not part of the angels that destroy the wicked in the Seven Last Plagues, since there are seven angels, not five. They also say that this slaying of the wicked within the church, which they say takes place during the

Little Time of Trouble before the Close of Probation, is a separate slaying from the general slaying of the wicked to take place in the course of the Great Time of Trouble during the plagues and Christ's Second Coming. They believe the wheat and tares in the Seventh-day Adventist Church will be separated during the Little Time of Trouble, and that the tares will be slain at that time. They believe the church must be purified and all the tares slain before the church can effectively preach the Third Angel's Message.

The truth of the matter is that the tares within the church are not destroyed separately during the Little Time of Trouble. Throughout the Spirit of Prophecy writings the wicked are all destroyed together by the plagues or the brightness of Jesus' Second Coming during the Great Time of Trouble. *The Great Controversy*, pp. 656, 657, makes a statement, contained in the following three paragraphs, which very aptly tells us when this destruction mentioned in Ezekiel 9 is to take place. *"The mark of deliverance has been set upon those 'that sigh and that cry for all the abominations that be done.' Now the angel of death goes forth, represented in Ezekiel's vision by the men with the slaughtering weapons, to whom the command is given: 'Slay utterly old and young, both maids, and little children, and women: but come not near any man upon whom is the mark; and begin at My sanctuary.' Says the prophet: 'They began at the ancient men which were before the house.'" Ezekiel 9:1-6. The work of destruction begins among those who have professed to be the spiritual guardians of the people. The false watchmen are the first to fall. There are none to pity or to spare. Men, women, maidens, and little children perish together.*

'The Lord cometh out of His place to punish the inhabitants of the earth for their iniquity: the earth also shall disclose her blood, and shall no more cover her slain.' Isaiah 26:21. 'And this shall be the plague wherewith the Lord will smite all the people that have fought against Jerusalem; Their flesh shall consume away while they stand upon their feet, and their eyes shall consume away in their holes, and their tongue shall consume away in their mouth. And it shall come to pass in that day, that a great tumult from the Lord shall be among them; and they shall lay hold everyone on the hand of his neighbor, and his hand shall rise up against the hand of his neighbor.' Zechariah 14:12, 13. In the mad strife of their own fierce passions, and by the

awful outpouring of God's unmingled wrath, fall the wicked inhabitants of the earth—priests, rulers, and people, rich and poor, high and low. 'And the slain of the Lord shall be at that day from one end of the earth even unto the other end of the earth: they shall not be lamented, neither gathered, nor buried.' Jeremiah 25:33.

At the coming of Christ the wicked are blotted from the face of the whole earth—consumed with the spirit of His mouth and destroyed by the brightness of His glory. Christ takes His people to the City of God, and the earth is emptied of its inhabitants. 'Behold, the Lord maketh the earth empty, and maketh it waste, and turneth it upside down, and scattereth abroad the inhabitants thereof.' 'The land shall be utterly emptied, and utterly spoiled: for the Lord hath spoken this word.' 'Because they have transgressed the laws, changed the ordinance, broken the everlasting covenant. Therefore hath the curse devoured the earth, and they that dwell therein are desolate: therefore the inhabitants of the earth are burned.' Isaiah 24:1, 3, 5, 6."

This statement puts the destruction of Ezekiel 9 at the outpouring of God's unmingled wrath. When does this occur? The answer to this question has been revealed in this book via Spirit of Prophecy writings. The outpouring of God's wrath mingled with mercy occurs during the Little Time of Trouble. The outpouring of God's wrath that is unmingled occurs during the Great Time of Trouble through the Seven Last Plagues, when probation has closed, especially during the seventh plague. This statement also clearly links the rest of the destruction in Ezekiel 9 to the destruction of individuals at the Second Coming of Christ.

In addition, the Spirit of Prophecy reveals to us that at this time these people rise up against each other. As revealed in Chapter 6, this occurs at the time of the seventh plague and the Second Coming of Christ. This is a time frame known as the general destruction of the wicked, when the wicked are destroyed either by each other, the seventh plague, or the brightness of the Second Coming of Christ. This passage does not indicate a destruction of the wicked in the church that is during the Little Time of Trouble and separate from the general destruction, as the Shepherd's Rod teaches. This passage links the destruction in Ezekiel 9 to the general destruction during the Great Time of Trouble. When allowing the Spirit of Prophecy to interpret itself, all statements must harmonize together, and, obviously, the Shepherd's Rod is taking statements out of context when compared to this statement and many others that follow.

From *Testimonies to Ministers and Gospel Workers*, pp. 431, 432, are the following two paragraphs: *"He who presides over His church and the destinies of nations is carrying forward the last work to be accomplished for this world. To His angels He gives the commission to execute His judgments. Let the ministers awake, let them take in the situation. The work of judgment begins at the sanctuary. 'And, behold, six men came from the way of the higher gate, which lieth toward the north, and every man a slaughter weapon in his hand; and one man among them was clothed with linen, with a writer's inkhorn by his side: and they went in, and stood beside the brazen altar.' Read Ezekiel 9:2-7. The command is, 'Slay utterly old and young, both maids, and little children, and women: but come not near any man upon whom is the mark; and begin at My sanctuary. Then they began at the ancient men which were before the house.' Saith God. 'I will recompense their way upon their head.'*

The words will soon be spoken, 'Go your ways, and pour out the vials of the wrath of God upon the earth.' One of the ministers of vengeance declares. 'And I heard the angel of the waters say, Thou art righteous, O Lord, which art, and wast, and shalt be, because Thou hast judged thus.' These heavenly beings, in executing the mandate of God, ask no questions, but do as they are bid. Jehovah of hosts, the Lord God Almighty, the just, the true, and the holy, has given them their work to do. With unswerving fidelity they go forth panoplied in pure white linen, having their breasts girded with golden girdles. And when their task is done, when the last vial of God's wrath is poured out, they return and lay their emptied vials at the feet of the Lord."

In this text the destruction of the wicked named in Ezekiel 9 is described as the pouring out of the vials of the wrath of God, and is therefore clearly linked to the Seven Last Plagues and the general destruction of the wicked, not some separate destruction for the wicked within the church, as promoted by the Shepherd's Rod. Again, they are taking certain biblical and Spirit of Prophecy passages and putting their own interpretation on them, without considering Spirit of Prophecy quotations such as this one, which clearly states that this destruction in Ezekiel 9 occurs during the Seven Last Plagues.

In *Testimonies to the Church*, Vol. 3, p. 267, is the following two paragraphs: *"Who are standing in the counsel of God at this time? Is it those who virtually excuse wrongs among the professed people of God and who murmur in their hearts, if not openly, against those who would reprove sin? Is it those who take their stand against them and sympathize with those who commit wrong? No, indeed! Unless they repent, and leave the work of Satan in oppressing those who have the burden of the work and in holding up the hands of sinners in Zion, they will never receive the mark of God's sealing approval. They will fall in the general destruction of the wicked, represented by the work of the five men bearing slaughter weapons. Mark this point with care: Those who receive the pure mark of truth, wrought in them by the power of the Holy Ghost, represented by a mark by the man in linen, are those 'that sigh and that cry for all the abominations that be done' in the church. Their love for purity and the honor and glory of God is such, and they have so clear a view of the exceeding sinfulness of sin, that they are represented as being in agony, even sighing and crying. Read the ninth chapter of Ezekiel.*

But the general slaughter of all those who do not thus see the wide contrast between sin and righteousness, and do not feel as those do who stand in the counsel of God and receive the mark, is described in the order to the five men with slaughter weapons: 'Go ye after him through the city, and smite: let not your eye spare, neither have ye pity: slay utterly old and young, both maids, and little children, and women: but come not near any man upon whom is the mark; and begin at My sanctuary.'"

Again, the destruction in Ezekiel 9 is clearly described as being the general destruction of the wicked during the Great Time of Trouble. How does the Shepherd's Rod justify taking passages from the Bible and Spirit of Prophecy and using them to suggest that there is a separate destruction of the wicked within the church, when that suggestion clearly conflicts with these texts and several others within the Spirit of Prophecy writings? This is a very clear example of not allowing the Spirit of Prophecy to interpret itself.

In Revelation 22:11, 12, Jesus tells us when the death of the wicked will occur. *"He that is unjust, let him be unjust still: and he which is filthy, let him be filthy still: and he that is righteous, let him be righteous still: and he that is holy, let him be holy still. And, behold, I come quickly; and my reward is with me, to give every man according as his work shall be."* In these verses we see that the Judgment of the Living has passed, probation has closed, and we are in the Great Time of Trouble. The reward is then given to the wicked and the righteous at the Second Coming of Christ, as Jesus brings the reward with Him. The reward is given to the righteous as they receive a new body and rise to meet the Lord in the air. However, the wicked receive their reward as they are destroyed by the seventh plague or the brightness of Jesus' Second Coming, both of which occur during the Second Coming of Jesus Christ. The wicked within the church are not destroyed in some special destruction prior to the Great Time of Trouble. All of mankind receives its reward as Jesus brings it with Him at His Second Coming.

In addition, how can the Shepherd's Rod say that the wheat and tares within the church will be separated during the Little Time of Trouble and the tares will be destroyed at that time, when we saw in Chapter 5 that tares are still in the church throughout the Great Time of Trouble during the Time of Jacob's Trouble?

The experience of the tares during the Time of Jacob's Trouble is described in *The Great Controversy*, p. 620. *"Those professed Christians who come up to that last fearful conflict [the Time of Jacob's Trouble] unprepared, will, in their despair, confess their sins in words of burning anguish, while the wicked exult over their distress."*

The experience of the tares is further described in *Signs of the Times*, Nov. 27, 1879. *"In these days of peril [the Great Time of Trouble] those who have been unfaithful in their duties in life, and whose mistakes and sins of neglect are registered against them in the book in Heaven, unrepented of and unforgiven, will be overcome by Satan... These will have no shelter in the time of Jacob's trouble. Their sins will then appear of such magnitude that they will have no confidence to pray, no heart to wrestle as did Jacob. On the other hand, those who have been of like passion, erring and sinful in their lives, but who have repented of their sins, and in genuine sorrow confessed them, will have pardon written against their names in the heavenly records. They will be hid in the day of the Lord's anger. Satan will attack this class, but like Jacob they have taken hold of the strength of God, and true to his character he is at peace with them, and sends angels to comfort and bless and sustain them in their time of peril."*

Notice that the Time of Jacob's Trouble occurs after the judgment has taken place. Pardon is written against the names of those that are saved. This text and others revealed in Chapter 5 place the Time of Jacob's Trouble during the Great Time of Trouble, and there are still tares in the church. As the Bible says, the wheat and tares do grow together until the harvest, the Second Coming of Christ, as revealed throughout this book.

The Shepherd's Rod, however, believes the harvest takes place during the Little Time of Trouble, which is a direct contradiction to previous passages and the following statement found in the *Review & Herald*, Jan. 10, 1893, from an article entitled "Let Both Grow Together": *"The tares are permitted to grow among the wheat, to have all the advantage of sun and shower; but in the time of the harvest, 'shall ye return, and discern between him that serveth God, and him that serveth him not;' for then every soul will be revealed in his true character. The tares will be bound into bundles to be burned, the wheat gathered into the heavenly garner."* This statement clearly puts the time of the harvest at the return of Jesus Christ.

As revealed above, many tares are shaken out of the church during the Little Time of Trouble, but there are still some that remain in the church during the Great Time of Trouble. However, the Shepherd's Rod promotes the belief that the tares within the church are all destroyed and the church is purified during the Little Time of Trouble. As revealed in the above passages, this is not true at all according to the Spirit of Prophecy and the Bible. The actual truth, as revealed throughout the biblical and Spirit of Prophecy writings, is that the remnant, the pure wheat, are purified, not the whole church. During the Little Time of Trouble, the majority of the tares are shaken out of the church and go to the world's side of the conflict. However, there are some tares that remain in the church even in the Time of Jacob's Trouble, which reaches its peak between the sixth and seventh plagues. They then have no confidence to pray as Jacob did, and they lose their way. All of the tares are then destroyed in the general destruction during the seventh plague and the Second Coming of Christ.

While the Shepherd's Rod utilizes Ezekiel 9, Isaiah 66, and Matthew 13, as well as Spirit of Prophecy passages to uphold the belief that the tares within the church are destroyed during the Little Time of Trouble, this belief cannot and should not be accepted because it contradicts a multitude of other Spirit of Prophecy texts and biblical passages, including those listed above that state that the destruction described in Ezekiel 9 takes place during the general destruction of the wicked, at the time of the seventh plague and the Second Coming of Christ.

In addition, there are many other passages that state that the majority of the lost within the church are shaken out of the church during the Little Time of Trouble, while there is nothing said about destruction. For example, in *Selected Messages*, Book 2, p. 380, is the following statement. "The church may appear as about to fall, but it does not fall. It remains, while the sinners in Zion will be sifted out—-the chaff separated from the precious wheat. This is a terrible ordeal, but nevertheless it must take place. None but those who have been overcoming by the blood of the Lamb and the word of their testimony will be found with the loyal and true, without spot or stain of sin, without guile in their mouths."

Again, we must allow the Spirit of Prophecy and the Bible to interpret themselves. God does not say to one prophet something that contradicts another prophet. He also does not say something to one prophet and contradict what He said to that prophet later on in another statement. It is only our understandings and interpretations of what is said that contradict.

What is being done by the Shepherd's Rod concerning their belief in the destruction of the wicked within the church during the Little Time of Trouble, is also done by the general Christian church concerning the State of the Dead. The general Christian church takes four texts out of the Bible to establish its belief that you go to heaven or hell as soon as you die. This interpretation of those four texts is completely out of harmony with the rest of the Bible, which indicates through more than thirty texts that you sleep in the grave until the resurrection. When this occurs and we are allowing the Bible to interpret itself, we must assume that there is something wrong with the interpretation and understanding of those four texts. Those four texts could actually be interpreted in such a way that they harmonize completely with the rest of the biblical passages.

Likewise, the three biblical passages as well as Spirit of Prophecy texts used by the Shepherd's Rod to establish their claim that the tares within the church are destroyed during the Little Time of Trouble is completely out of harmony with numerous biblical and Spirit of Prophecy texts. These texts state that the tares are destroyed in the general destruction of the wicked in the Great Time of Trouble, during the outpouring of God's wrath in the seventh plague and during the Second Coming of Christ. Therefore, the Shepherd's Rod interpretation of their biblical and Spirit of Prophecy passages cannot be correct. When allowing the Bible and Spirit of Prophecy to interpret themselves, and the texts that support their position are in direct contradiction to a vast number of texts throughout the Spirit of Prophecy and the Bible, it must be assumed that there is something wrong with their understanding and interpretation of those texts. It is possible that those texts could be interpreted and understood in such a way that they would harmonize with the rest of the Bible and Spirit of Prophecy passages that state that the tares within the church are destroyed during the general destruction of the wicked at the seventh plague and Second Coming of Christ. This would be the ultimate demonstration of allowing the Bible and Spirit of Prophecy texts to interpret themselves. Even so, when the few are in direct contradiction to the majority, it must be assumed that the majority is correct, when allowing the Bible and Spirit of Prophecy to interpret themselves, and that there is something wrong with our understanding of the few.

In closing, the main message I want to convey is that when dealing with groups such as the Shepherd's Rod, that routinely interpret Spirit of Prophecy and biblical passages for themselves, without regard to the other Spirit of Prophecy and biblical texts concerning the same subject, please be careful to study before and after those texts they cite and study all of the passages you can find concerning that same subject to obtain a correct understanding and interpretation of their text. By allowing the Bible and the Spirit of Prophecy to interpret themselves, we can ensure that we will not be deceived, and will be better prepared for the Second Coming of Jesus Christ!

About the Author

Kerry L. Schoonmaker began his life-long passion for spreading the good news of the Gospel as soon as he was baptized in Philipsburg, NJ in 1975. He was quickly ordained a deacon, and then conducted seminars to stop smoking, taught vegetarian cooking classes, created the Encounter Correspondence Bible School, and brought a number of people to the foot of the Cross. Continuing with his passion, he founded Christianity, Inc. in 1986. This non-profit 501-C-3 corporation is dedicated to spreading the gospel by all means possible including public meetings, cassette programs and the written word. He honed his evangelistic skills with training by Joe Crews and Louis Torres of Amazing Facts TV/radio program. This led to a number of successful evangelistic campaigns. By 1995 Kerry became the speaker/director of "The Bible Hotline," answering questions live on WDVR in New Jersey. Turning next to sharing his evangelistic expertise with fellow believers Kerry created seminars on how to persuasively present the Three Angels' Messages and how to properly understand Final Events. At this time he developed a "Marking the Bible" program by creating a 118 page manual enabling believers to mark their Bibles on 40 different subjects. Included in his creative endeavors is the development of two 6-cassette programs entitled "The Anti-Christ, the False Prophet, and the Whore Babylon Revealed", "The Final Events," which led to this book, and a single cassette titled "What Really Happens After Death". Kerry continues to preach, teach and carry out His Lord's commission to spread the word.

We invite you to view the complete
selection of titles we publish at:

www.LNFBooks.com

or write or email us your praises,
reactions, or thoughs about this
or any other book we publish at:

TEACH Services, Inc.
P.O. Box 954
Ringgold, GA 30736

info@TEACHServices.com